OTHER HAY HOUSE TITLES
OF RELATED INTEREST

BOOKS

Adventures of a Psychic, by Sylvia Browne
Chakra Clearing, by Doreen Virtue, Ph.D.
Conversations with the Other Side, by Sylvia Browne
*Crossing Over, by John Edward
Diary of a Psychic, by Sonia Choquette (coming in July 2003)

AUDIO PROGRAMS

Angels and Spirit Guides, by Sylvia Browne
*Developing Your Own Psychic Powers, by John Edward
Making Contact with the Other Side, by Sylvia Browne
Unleashing Your Psychic Potential, by John Edward
Understanding Your Angels and Meeting Your Guides,
by John Edward

CARD DECKS

Heart and Soul, by Sylvia Browne
Healing with the Angels Oracle Cards, by Doreen Virtue, Ph.D.
Messages from Your Angels Oracle Cards, by Doreen Virtue, Ph.D.
Miracle Cards, by Marianne Williamson

All of the above are available at your local bookstore,
or may be ordered through Hay House, Inc.:

(800) 654-5126 or **(760) 431-7695**
(800) 650-5115 (fax) or **(760) 431-6948 (fax)**
www.hayhouse.com

*Published by Princess Books; distributed by Hay House

born KNOWING

A Medium's Journey—Accepting and Embracing My Spiritual Gifts

John Holland

with Cindy Pearlman

Hay House, Inc.
Carlsbad, California • Sydney, Australia
Canada • Hong Kong • United Kingdom

Published and distributed in the United States by: Hay House, Inc., P.O. Box 5100, Carlsbad, CA 92018-5100 • (760) 431-7695 or (800) 654-5126 • (760) 431-6948 (fax) or (800) 650-5115 (fax) • www.hayhouse.com • **Published and distributed in Australia by:** Hay House Australia Pty Ltd, P.O. Box 515, Brighton-Le-Sands, NSW 2216 • *phone:* 1800 023 516 • *e-mail:* info@hayhouse.com.au • **Distributed in the United Kingdom by:** Airlift, 8 The Arena, Mollison Ave., Enfield, Middlesex, United Kingdom EN3 7NL • **Distributed in Canada by:** Raincoast, 9050 Shaughnessy St., Vancouver, B.C., Canada V6P 6E5

Editorial supervision: Jill Kramer   *Design:* Amy Rose Szalkiewicz

Library of Congress Cataloging-in-Publication Data

Holland, John
Born knowing : a medium's journey—accepting and embracing my spiritual gifts / John Holland with Cindy Pearlman.
    p. cm.
ISBN 1-40190-082-8 (tradepaper)
    1. Holland, John, 1961- 2. Mediums—United States—Biography.
I. Pearlman, Cindy, 1964- II. Title.
      BF1283.H65 A3 2003
      133.9'1'092—dc21

                  2002152964

            ISBN 1-4019-0082-8

      06 05 04 03   4 3 2 1
      1st printing, March 2003

            Printed in Canada

To Jennie,
My Angel on Earth

Set a dream before you,
If the dream can be shared,
Watch it become a reality.
— John Holland

CONTENTS

PREFACE

Balloons to Heaven

ANGELS DON'T JUST SING—
they also dance.

In my head, I could hear someone gliding across a polished wooden floor. But I was confused—this wasn't the familiar rhythm of a waltz. It sounded more like *clackity-clack, clackity-clack, clackity-clack.* Heaven was tap dancing.

"Did Jennifer have a pair of tap shoes?" I asked her mother, Melinda, whose eyes instantly filled with tears. I could tell that once again, I'd succeeded in becoming a conduit for someone from the Other Side.

This time, the person reaching out was Jennifer, Melinda's five-year-old daughter, who had crossed to the Other Side after a kidney operation went tragically wrong. Jennifer had died on Father's Day, during the one hour that the hospital staff had begged her family to "go home, relax, and get something to eat" because nothing would happen. Yet something tremendous *did* happen, and the first one to know was Lisa, Jennifer's seven-year-old sister, who was running through the overgrown grass in the front yard at the exact moment Jennifer passed on. Her parents found Lisa pointing upwards and crying, "See! My sister! My sister!" to a small white butterfly that swooped down and slowly circled over Lisa's head.

Three years had since passed, and Melinda needed to know if her baby was safe in heaven. So she decided to call a medium. I wanted so terribly to give her some answers, but at first I felt frustrated, as I couldn't see or feel Jennifer. Instead, I just kept hearing the same noise, over and over . . . *clackity-clack, clackity-clack, clackity-clack.*

I realized that I couldn't ignore the sound any longer, so that's when I asked Melinda if Jennifer took tap-dancing lessons.

Melinda started weeping. "No, but I understand the sound," she whispered. "The Christmas before Jennifer died, she received a pair of clogs that had a metal heel on them that tapped when she walked."

It seemed that the shoes were too big for Jennifer's little feet, but she insisted on wearing them anyway—even though they almost fell off with a clacking thud every time she walked. In fact, Jennifer loved those shoes so much that she'd beg to visit her aunt (who worked in a hospital with hard wooden floors), so she could skip down the long corridors for maximum effect. She adored the sound of the *clackity-clack* noise, which echoed down the hallways. She'd giggle and ask Melinda: "Do you hear me making the noise, Mommy?"

Melinda told me that Jennifer had been buried in those shoes . . . and I heard her dancing in heaven.

Before she faded away, Jennifer had a message for her mother: "Please tell Mommy that it doesn't hurt anymore, and I love the balloons."

I expressed this to Melinda, who was by now speechless. Finally, she pulled herself together and said, "On the anniversary of Jennifer's death, and on her birthday each year, we stuff balloons with a message for her and release them into the sky. We put her name with her photo on each and every balloon."

She paused and asked, "John, how could you know all that?"

I've always known that I came into this world with a special gift. It was as though I was somehow . . . born knowing.

ACKNOWLEDGMENTS

FIRST, I HAVE TO THANK GOD, Spirit, my Higher Power, "my team" that works with me on the Other Side; and all my family and friends on this side of life.

Thank you to all the mediums who have gone before me for setting the standards for this work.

A special thanks to all my clients who were willing to share their personal and often private stories for this book. Their experiences will touch many hearts that are in need of healing.

And thanks specifically to:

Joyce, for seeing a talent that could help so many. I'm so grateful for your friendship and encouragement, and for pushing me out of the nest. Your trusting friendship has been, and always will be, one of my most treasured.

Simon, thank you! You're one of the kindest people on Earth, the rock that kept me grounded. And thank you for teaching me to see through new eyes, and for letting me know that it's okay to spread my wings and fly.

Gretchen Harb, my assistant, who helps structure and organize my busy schedule, thank you for all your hard work, your sense of humor and friendship, and for being there for so many of my clients.

Lynn Robinson: Sharing and speaking with you has always given me the inspiration and courage to make a difference. I'll always admire your constant support, professionalism, and most of all, your enthusiasm.

Cindy Pearlman, for being my writing partner and for your contribution in turning a life into a story.

John Willig, my agent. Thanks for your listening ear—thank God you have two!—and for all of your help, professionalism, advice, and sense of humor; and for your work in helping to spread the word.

Suzane Northrop: A BIG thank you for reaching out to me when I *really* needed it. Your friendship, professionalism, and integrity has only helped me to help others. I'm glad you're in my life. Every medium needs a good medium, but more important, they need a friend who understands.

Judy Guggenheim: Thanks for all your support, not just for myself, but for the thousands that you've touched with Bill's and your research.

Edy Nathan: Thank you for your counseling skills and for your contribution to this book. Watching you work with people and the compassion you so freely give is and always will be a learning experience for my soul.

John Edward: Thanks to you and Carol for all your support, and for going out on a limb for us all.

The Hay House family: Thank you all for having the knowledge and compassion to help and educate the masses. Your hard work, enthusiasm, guidance, and support on *Born Knowing* will always be greatly appreciated.

I also want to acknowledge the following people, for no man can ever truly do it all by himself. Your friendship and support has never been forgotten: Cosgrove Meurer Productions; Judy Guggenheim, a true ambassador for Spirit; Jordon Rich, WBZ Radio, for support and for putting a little *spirit* into the airwaves; Cathy and the staff at Circles of Wisdom; Randall and Elizabeth Hermon and the staff of The 9th House; Unicorn Bookstore and Kathy Schregardus for always being ready to help; Seven Stars Bookstore; Diana, Rosa, and the staff of Center for Balance; Anne Marie and everyone at Conscious Living, WA; Clint Connolly at Chronicle; Jennifer Vaughn and the staff of WMUR; Debbie Luican; Lorna Brunell and staff at The Burt Wood School; Improper Bostonian, Joe Chapple, at BCAE, IntuitiveVision; Talk Radio; Boston Learning Society; Patrick Gerbier for your beautiful art; Debbie Eriksen (a friend forever and then some); Craig Hughes; Darlene Bethoney; Joel Idelson; Patty M.; Rina; Samm Bogues; Peter Serraino; Chris and Paul; Jenay; Jodi; Leslie R.; Dilek; Mo; Lisa; Bob and Melissa Olson; Bob and Annie Smythe; Adrian Coros; Maury; Cathy Copeland; Kate and Yanick; Sue; Margo Brooks; Lesley Osborne; Vincent J. Barra; Richie B. and Lisa; JJSH; Holly; Josie and Des; Mei-Mei; Josie J.; Regine; The Consulate; Dave; Randy; Vern; T.L.; Mary Margarita; Linda Manning; Clarke and Sue; Buck Beaudoin; and all the family and friends who've supported me.

In England, I met some truly amazing people. I'd like to thank you all for your friendship and guidance, for opening up your homes as well as your hearts, and for taking me under so many of your wings: Margert Stanley and The Devizers Spiritualist Church; Joan Lambert; Gordon Smith; Jim Dronma; Westbury Park Spiritualist Church and my Brislington Circle; Jean; Diane; Marion; John; Mary (of course) for making sure I always had a friend and a ride to experience it all with; Peter Close; the S.A.G.B.; Eric and Pam Beer; and all my tutors at Arthur Findlay College.

— ◉ —

INTRODUCTION
My Life As a Medium

LOOKING BACK ON MY EARLY YEARS, I guess learning to walk, speak, and eat (along with many of the other normal requirements of life) was a breeze compared to the real lessons I'd end up having to master.

I often joke that when I was born, it wasn't as though I shot out with an instruction manual titled *How to Grow Up and Become a Medium.* No, I was just a normal kid growing up in Boston, where I dealt with the happiness and sadness that were both a part of my early life. I felt like most other kids, but the truth of the matter is that I was different in the best way possible.

I don't want to give the impression that my early years were carefree, because they weren't. I didn't get to enjoy family vacations like so many other kids my age or watch my parents relax and stop working. Instead, I had to grow up quickly due to a disease in our family (more on that later) that forced me to take on the parental role of guardian and protector. This created an atmosphere with little guidance and even less support. When I discovered that I was, in fact, "different," I couldn't really turn to my mom or dad. I had to stand tall and find my way on my own. My life was enhanced because I realized at a very young age that human beings don't just have five senses—we actually have another that we're all born with, but we forget that it's there. I'm talking about our sixth (psychic) sense.

So many of us run away from what we were born to do. I stopped running. The book you're about to read explains how I came to terms with such a misunderstood ability. After all, if someone had told me that one day I'd be standing on a stage in front of hundreds of people—without any props, scenery, or scripts—I would have thought that they were out of their minds.

Well, that's exactly how my life has turned out . . . but it hasn't been an easy journey. I've come far and experienced great growth, but most important, I've been taught priceless lessons. I've written this book to pass on those lessons and provide inspiration to those who may have similar challenges ahead of them.

◎

This book is deliberately written in a no-holds-barred style. The first part of *Born Knowing* tells the story of how I struggled to accept my gift of mediumship. The second part deals with clients' personal stories, which are offered with the hope that they'll assist someone else who's hurting or who might need inspiration in dealing with a loss (and I'm so grateful for these brave people who shared their most personal moments with me). The last part of the book is about how I embraced the work, and it will allow you to see what it's like to be a medium. I'll show you how Spirit influences our lives, because our loved ones are always connected to us. And I'll also offer a few simple lessons that will help you begin to develop your own forgotten abilities and assist you in your own awareness.

This book isn't just about communicating with those who have passed. It's also about life, and the incredible spiritual powers and potential we possess as humans. And just like life, I want this book to be an education. If I can help point you in a spiritual direction, if I've shaved off some time in your search by providing information, or if you read something that makes you question and then go on your own investigation and research, then I'll feel that I've done my job.

part I

my EARLY life

chapter 1

THE LIGHT

"COME ON, JOHNNY! LET'S GO!" screamed my older brother Danny as he ripped the dusty book out of my hands and tossed my torn Red Sox cap into my lap. "The guys are waiting!"

His last words sounded as if they were coming from very far away because he was halfway out the door when he said them. When I heard the smack of the metal screen door, I knew that I only had a few minutes to decide whether to remain inside the small apartment or join the other kids outside on this perfect summer day.

Looking out the window, I smiled at the sight of the other neighborhood boys, but I couldn't help but feel a bit torn. My little eight-year-old body didn't want to move, for the best reason in the world: I was working my mind, and I was about to turn the yellowed page of another one of my metaphysical books.

I was always checking these books out of the library, despite the quizzical look on the librarian's face. "Most boys your age like to read about cars or sports," she told me.

I'd ignore her helpful suggestions as I lifted volume after volume on theological studies, dreams, or ghosts onto the counter. There was only one problem—these tomes were generally so heavy that I actually wobbled when I carried them home. Every few blocks, I'd have to put them down so I could catch my breath.

On this particular day, I was happily surrounded by my books. In fact, part of me felt like it would burst if it couldn't get to the information on the next page as soon as possible. It was as if some teacher in my head was telling me that today's lesson was not quite complete. I shook my head as I tried to figure it all out. It was true that I got A's and B's on my report cards at school, but devouring books at the college level while I was on summer vacation was another story. Most kids my age would have just been happy looking at the pictures, but I craved the words and the knowledge. The only problem was that this was a sunny day in June—75 degrees with a cool breeze and endless possibilities.

On an impulse, the average kid in me took over as I leapt off the bed, nearly tripping on the shoelaces I rarely tied. I could read later, right? It was summer vacation, and I was going to make the most of it.

◎

It was June 1973, in Dorchester, Massachusetts—a working-class suburb of Boston that had seen better days. It seemed that my hometown had become a "before-and-after" advertisement right before my very eyes. A few years ago, Dorchester had been an overcrowded but well-kept part of the world, where men who "scraped their pennies together" got up at dawn and trudged off to jobs that provided necessities but few luxuries for their families. Still, they told their children that it was the best that they could do.

But a force greater than the collective optimism in the neighborhood had chipped away this "can do" mentality. Times were tight, and several families had been forced to move to new cities in search of better opportunities. The helplessness of poverty settled over the town like a heavy fog that just wouldn't lift, leaving a new level of sadness that only children in their innocence could overlook.

I knew that the world was a big place, and the adventures I longed for were just around the corner. I also knew that living in Dorchester wasn't going to be my destiny . . . but while I *was* there, I might as well get some enjoyment out of life's simple pleasures. I was a normal kid with sneakers that could go thousands of miles, and an imagination that was limitless.

"Look who's here!" my friend Billy said as I walked outside. "Finally! Let's get going!" Then he yelled up the block: "Hey, Danny, your brother the hermit is actually out in the sunlight. Think he'll melt?" There was no time to answer that one because there were big plans in motion. We had the entire Saturday to see what kind of mischief could be found.

"Let's go to the girls' school," Billy exclaimed, leading the way before anyone could outvote him. Two streets over was the all-brick school, which was a great place to hang out because there were no grown-ups around on the weekends. It was just kids, some tall grass, and a wall to keep things private. There was only one glitch when it came to our personal Shangri-la: Over in one corner of the school, there was a steep slope leading down to where the school janitors parked their trucks. The sign made it clear that it was a major "Keep-Out

Zone," and even my fearless friends seemed to realize it was dangerous as they chose to race each other to the wall.

Everyone was running—except for me. I stopped for a reason that I couldn't really explain to the others. How could I tell them that I felt drawn to another place? The slope was calling to me, and it was as if invisible hands were gently guiding me in that direction.

"Go down there, Johnny," a voice in my head said. Suddenly, and without a second thought, I was sliding down the slippery concrete in the direction of the "Keep-Out Zone." A few seconds later, the other kids noticed what I was doing and came over to stop me, but there was no turning back. I was halfway down the hill.

"He's got a screw loose!" screamed Billy.

Even my brother was nervous. "Hey, Johnny, get your ass back up here or I'm gonna tell Mom!" Danny yelled.

I ignored his frantic tones as the voice in my head grew louder. *"Keep going,"* it insisted.

My buddies stayed up at the fenceline while I climbed farther down the slope, choosing to shimmy down the grassy area next to the concrete because I could get down there quicker. As I got near the bottom, I tripped and tumbled the last few feet. I didn't care about my torn jeans or my now-dirty hands, which were used again and again to break my fall. My father was going to kill me for ruining my one good pair of jeans, but I simply couldn't stop my feet from moving ahead.

When I reached the level ground at the bottom, I glanced back up at my friends, who now seemed far away, but I wasn't afraid. *"Don't stop now, Johnny,"* said the voice. Soon, I was at the opening where the janitors parked their trucks. Willing my feet to walk inside this private cave, I suddenly found myself in damp, dark territory, where I could actually hear the stillness of the humid air. The only light was a tiny stream of muted sunshine, which created a faint glow inside.

I was guided to a young man who was curled up on the concrete in a pool of his own blood. His body was outlined in shards of glass that glittered like hundreds of sparkling diamonds. I realized that he was hurt, and my guess was that he must have fallen off the landing above us. Somehow I knew he wasn't dead, but as I got closer, I could tell that his breathing was shallow, and he was seriously injured. I don't know how, but I also knew something else: His soul was somehow calling out to me for help.

As tears rolled down my face, I summoned up the strength to run up the slope with all the speed that my skinny legs could muster, and I didn't stop until I was home again. I burst inside and lifted the phone with shaking hands.

"What's wrong, honey?" my mom called out from the kitchen.

I couldn't answer her, for at the time I was saying to the operator: "Hello, give me the police. It's an emergency!"

That night I opened the door to find a burly police officer standing there. He asked to see my parents, but I wasn't in trouble. Instead, he'd come to thank me. It turned out that the officer was the uncle of the young man who fell. "Your boy is a hero," the policeman told my incredulous parents. The officer then proceeded to fill us in on what had happened. "My nephew passed away this evening, but at least he wasn't alone. His entire family was with him and got to say goodbye." Putting his large hand on my shoulder, the teary-eyed man said, "Thank you, son." And then he put his head down in sadness and slowly walked away.

My family never talked about what happened that day.

People are always asking me when or how I first knew I was psychic. I can't pinpoint the exact moment, but I'd felt it long before I discovered that hurting soul in the janitor's cave.

Looking back, the first time I can remember something phenomenal was when I was about six or seven. It was definitely past midnight, so my bedroom was quite dark. I'd woken up for no apparent reason and glanced at my two brothers who were asleep on the far side of the tiny, crowded room. Straining my eyes in the darkness to familiarize myself with my surroundings, I was comforted by the peeling '60s-style green wallpaper I'd seen my entire life. As usual, clothes and toys were scattered all over the floor, which seemed very normal to me. Yet I shivered slightly as I felt the room's temperature drop. What was going on?

Something was in the room. I could sense its presence, and then it made itself known. I was confused and fascinated, but surprisingly, I wasn't scared. Out of the corner of my eye, I was drawn to a small spark of light dancing in the air. Was it the reflection of a headlight coming through the window, or the flickering streetlight? No, it was too tiny—it reminded me of a small pocket penlight, for it was just the smallest speck of illumination flitting about the room. Suddenly, it was as though the outside world had suddenly ceased to exist, and I couldn't hear a thing. I was frozen in the moment.

The light gathered speed as I watched it bounce from one wall to another. I tried to figure out where it had come from, but there was no time to think. Soon, the light was hovering in front of my face, and before I could move or turn away, it seemed to shoot right through me. It felt like an exploding star, and it made my entire body vibrate. Every cell seemed to be charged with energy.

I knew that most kids would have crawled under their beds or screamed for their mothers, so it was strange that I wasn't afraid. As a matter of fact, I felt illuminated from the inside out, even though my practical voice of reasoning was screaming, *What was that?!*

I turned around in my bed to see where the light was, but just as quickly as it had arrived, it vanished. As my mind returned to a semblance of consciousness, I remained upright for some time until my body slowly calmed down. As I pulled the blankets up even higher around me, I realized one thing—sleep was out of the question.

Then another difficult question popped into my young mind: *Whom could I possibly tell? Who would believe me?*

chapter 2

TRAINING WHEELS

WHEN I WAS A CHILD, I'D OFTEN find my mother slumped wearily on the couch in the afternoons, recuperating from her previous night at the local pizzeria and contemplating another eight-hour shift later that day. I'd slide in next to her, hoping to give her some comfort . . . but really wanting some attention, too.

She'd pretend not to see me at first, but then I'd see the twinkle in her dark brown eyes. A slow smile would creep across her face, which showed the strain of her life's struggles. Even so, her smile was my signal to begin. Our game was *on.*

"Come on, Ma," I'd say. "Pick a color." It was easy to know if she'd chosen green or red, but when I came up with words such as *turquoise* or *burgundy,* she'd give me one of her incredulous looks.

I was rarely wrong in our no-stakes guessing game, but I didn't think too much of it at the time. When colors became boring, we'd move on to numbers and letters. As time wore on, I got better and better at this game—it was strange that here I was indoors practicing my own "sport," while other kids were perfecting their batting technique for the street baseball games. Now I sometimes wonder, *Was I just practicing? Or was I somehow remembering and fine-tuning skills from another time?*

When my mother would drag us kids out for our regular shots, it was another opportunity for me to practice—and my brothers and sisters loved it. In the main entrance to the hospital, I'd play the "elevator game," which meant that we stood in front of three elevator doors and I'd try to choose which one would open first. "Right again, Johnny," my brother Danny would say, rolling his eyes in amazement. I tried to get my siblings to stay with me as long as possible so I could see how many times I got it right.

Sometimes my mother took me shopping with her, and my favorite department store was Filene's because they had an automatic door. I'd pretend that my mind was able to make the door open and close, as if the entire thing was magic. My mother was forever patient with me, letting me indulge myself time after time.

I'm sure other kids on the block would have considered my games weird—in fact, some of them liked to call me "freak"—but it seemed like normal childhood stuff to my siblings and me. There were other times, however, when my childhood wasn't normal at all. For instance, on some evenings when I'd lie awake in bed, I'd see "the spirit people"—shadowy figures with the kindest faces and an illumination around them—walking through my bedroom. From my first encounter with them, I knew that they weren't there to scare me; in fact, they went out of their way to look at me warmly, or simply nod a quick hello. I didn't know who these people were, but I felt strangely comforted and protected by their presence. Of course, I never told anyone about these visits, but I made a mental plan to figure it out for myself someday.

I searched for answers like a scientist trying to discover a new vaccine. Always examining everything minutely, I was forever probing and analyzing. Perhaps I didn't want to simply accept this strange gift without getting inside it first.

My first step was to grill my mother about my birth. I'd read in one of my many books that babies born with a gauze-like layer of skin (known as a *caul*) over their faces will be psychic, but that was also known as an old wives' tale. And so, I wanted to know every detail of my birth: Were the planets in some sort of alignment? Had another psychic predicted that she'd give birth to a son or that this baby would possess something a little more than most people?

My mother didn't have any stunning revelations to pass on to me, as I was just another normal seven-pound baby boy born to Irish-Italian, Catholic parents who didn't seem to have anything mystical in their pasts. My mom and dad had met at a local bakery, and the beautiful Italian woman with jet-black hair fell in love with the handsome, redheaded, Irish ex-Marine. I believe it was a real case of love at first sight.

Ma and Dad married after a three-month courtship and moved into a small three-bedroom apartment to begin their new life. Five children followed in rapid succession, almost exactly a calender year apart. The struggle to support all of us wore heavily on my father, and after a while, my parents seemed to lose the hope that was their shining light when they were younger. My siblings and I didn't know where our folks turned for strength or help . . . but we soon realized that my father's source of comfort was a liquid one.

As the years wore on, my father began to drink more heavily, but that wasn't the only problem facing our family. Not only were *we* struggling, but the entire city of Dorchester was rapidly becoming a slum because the state was making little or no investment in the area. Our neighbors moved away from their little homes; consequently, the dwellings quickly became vacant shells covered in graffiti. It became dangerous for women to walk around at night, but my mother had little choice. Since we needed the money, she found work at the local pizzeria as a cook in the evenings. My father was supposed to look after us, but we were stuck with a man who had a few demons of his own—ones that simply wouldn't go away.

These conditions made me grow up quicker than most other kids; I also took on the responsibility of helping to raise my younger siblings, who suffered in silence when it came to my father's drinking (as did my mother). Being in an alcoholic home, it helped to know what was in store for us. So it was during this time that my greatest support and comfort was my ability to know things ahead of time. . . .

Yet, even during these difficult and anxious times, my family did experience moments of pure joy. Our summers weren't about going to a beach house or popping up the picnic umbrella—they were taken up with simple pleasures, such as cold showers in the street when the temperature soared to over 90 degrees. Some of the neighborhood kids would unscrew the cap off a fire hydrant and bask under the full force of our instant cooling fountain. We'd scream in delight as we drenched ourselves in the spray, as the swollen, black-tarred streets buckled and bubbled in the heat. For my brothers and sisters and me, the water and steaming roadways were enough to create some much-needed fun and laughter. I also enjoyed visiting the swan boats in Boston—vessels shaped like beautiful birds that sailed across a pond filled with real swans. That fun came for the price of a dollar a trip.

One of my regular escapes from this world was when I sat on the floor, legs crossed like a yogi, in front of our small black-and-white TV to watch *Bewitched* and *Night Gallery*. Another favorite was a gothic soap opera called *Dark Shadows*. That was the best!

I needed these little episodes because happiness at home was rare. I always dreaded Dad coming home, especially if he found me curled up with one of my books. He'd burst into the room, catching me off-guard and without a few minutes to hide my hobby under the couch. "You're weird, Johnny," he'd say, clearly disappointed that his boy was sitting there with his face glued to some old thing he borrowed from the library. I could hear the irritation in his sharp tone. "You should be outside playing baseball with the other kids, not stuck in here reading like some recluse!" On good days (that is, when he didn't want to hurt my feelings even more), he'd switch to just calling me "the different one."

I'd attempt to explain to him how I just saw things, but I don't think he was listening or interested. It seemed that my strange habits really annoyed him. "Stop it!" he'd yell. "You and that stupid imagination of yours!" He'd turn his back on me and find my mother, who was always nearby. She was just as helpless as I was, and she'd look down when he'd scowl and mumble, "There's something wrong with *your* son." So I tried to push my abilities down in some lame attempt to prevent my father from being upset with me.

In an odd twist, Dad did encourage me when he noticed that I had some aptitude for art—my drawings and paintings were certainly different from those of other kids my age.

My love for picking up the brushes, which bordered on obsession, meant that in the wee hours of the night, you could find me hiding under the bedcovers, drawing by the light of the small bedside lamp I hid under the sheets.

My hands sketched images, symbols, people, and places that I realized I'd never known. They weren't scenes from some TV show or one of my many books, yet somehow they were strangely familiar, as though I was meant to draw them. I'd wonder, *Where did they come from? Was it my imagination or subconscious? Why do I draw so many pictures of children playing with angels?*

I knew that no one on my father's side shared any of the abilities that bothered him so much, but my mother's family was a different story—and I quickly realized that it would be worth finding out as much as I could about them. A few times a year my mother and I would go to my grandmother's house to bask in the peace and serenity that was always present in her modest but immaculately clean house.

Grandma Rose had many of the same gifts I possessed, but at first glance, you couldn't tell that anything was remarkably different about her. She was a small, robust Italian woman who was always cooking and making homemade sauces. Being a rather highly strung kid, weight gain eluded me no matter how much I ate. So naturally, my grandmother felt obliged to feed me at every opportunity. The force-feedings were worth it because I got to be in her warm presence.

One of the things I especially loved about going to her house was looking at the old, faded photos on the walls, which provided a rare glimpse into the lives of some of distant relatives I'd never met, including my grandfather, whose name I shared. And I was transfixed by the statues of religious icons that seemed to be calling to me as I made my way down the dimly lit hallway. It was so peaceful in Grandma's bedroom, and I loved to just curl up on her bed and drift off into a calm, beautiful sleep. For those precious moments, everything in my world was close to normal. And then, on my way out the door, she'd often stick a dollar or two in my hand and whisper, "Don't tell anyone, Johnny, but you're special." Of course, I never did.

My Aunt Shirley, who lived with my grandmother, was another powerful influence in my life. She'd talk to me about the power of dreams, and show me the shelves in her room that were stacked with books on the subject, which discussed the meaning of dreams and exactly where our minds took us during slumber. I didn't know it then, but these were some of my first experiences and conversations about psychic matters. Shirley was also a fellow explorer in these uncharted waters that were rapidly becoming so familiar to me. She often joked that she used her dreams and books to play the lottery. Whether it was luck or psychic powers, she was damn good at it. Now I'm not advising anyone who thinks they have psychic ability to go out and start gambling, but this was just her way.

(As an aside, I'd just like to say that for years I've kept dream journals beside my bed for those little trips we take at night. So often, I realize how places and circumstances that first appeared in my dreams later become reality. I let my dreams sort out the clutter in my mind, and I generally wake up feeling clearer, because somehow the answers to my questions have come to me during the night.)

In those days of learning, exploration, and personal growth, Grandma and Aunt Shirley were just known as "Rose" and "Shirley" to the rest of the family. They were accepted for the way they were, and we didn't question or try to label them—they were just "naturally intuitive." Of course, their abilities were hardly ever discussed, nor was "psychic" ever used to describe them.

Neither my grandmother nor my aunt attached any stigma to what they did—it didn't conflict with our family's Roman Catholic religious beliefs, and I suppose it was quite natural for them to use their intuition in their everyday lives. As a young boy, I wondered how the abilities I shared with my grandmother and aunt could blend with what I heard in church on Sundays, but then I learned that the Bible talks about the gifts of spirit. Although the word *psychic* is never mentioned, I was fascinated that the Bible talked about people who were given extraordinary abilities from God. *Yep, that's me,* I figured.

Grandma and Aunt Shirley probably didn't even realize they were special—yet clearly they were. Of course, there were things that we aren't supposed to know, but strangely, they *did.* For example, Shirley developed cancer and knew that she'd cross over on St. Patrick's Day. And just as she predicted, Shirley passed in her sleep on March 17.

Rose lived to be 98 years old and was very independent right up into her early 90s. One day I went to visit her in a nursing home, and she took my face in her hands, looked into my eyes, kissed me, and said, "Johnny, I will always love you."

I knew that this would be the last time I'd see her—at least in this world—and I was right. A few days later, my mother went to visit her. Mom said that my barely conscious grandmother reached up into the air with her frail arms, as if to grab on to invisible hands; she also called out to her husband and Shirley. She passed peacefully the following day, with a tranquil smile on her face.

I'd eventually learn that what Grandma Rose experienced frequently happens just before a person is about to pass. Today, I talk about these beautiful visions (known as *deathbed visions*) in my lectures and demonstrations, telling audiences that we never go home alone, because those who have gone before us will come to take our hands and help us on our journey.

Even though I'm a medium, I miss the fact that Rose and Shirley aren't here in the physical world. I long for them, realizing how much I needed them as psychic role models when I was a child. These days, I advise parents to really listen to a sensitive, "knowing" child who may claim that they're seeing or feeling things. Yes, it could be their overactive imagination, but it doesn't hurt to ask *what* they're seeing and feeling. If they're seeing a grandparent or someone who has passed—even if it's someone they've never met—ask, "What do they look like? What are they saying?" You might be very surprised. Listen to what comes out of the mouth of babes.

In actuality, *all* children are very sensitive—they're born quite aware, and haven't yet been told that they're not supposed to be. This sixth sense is just as necessary as the other five when we first come into this world—it's almost like a tool to help us during our stay here on Earth. Yet some children who have been ridiculed for their abilities will push their thoughts and feelings away, while others don't know what to do with them. Some children simply forget, and their abilities will fade away when they start school. They'll begin to use more of the left, analytical side of their brain, and the creative, intuitive right side will take a backseat.

Thankfully, today there's more information to encourage parents whose children are showing signs of a keen intuition. Psychic ability doesn't have to be something hidden, tucked away, and not talked about. It's really quite natural.

I've often reminisced about my childhood, trying to figure out why I wasn't totally shocked by some of the strange events I experienced. After all, when my friends today hear what happened to me, their eyes widen in amazement as they ask, "But you were just a boy. Weren't you afraid?"

"Honestly, how could I be frightened of something that was always there?" I retort.

Naturally, there were some events that *did* catch me off-guard.

One night I looked out my bedroom window and saw that the sky was glowing bright orange. At first, I thought that I was having one of my all-too-vivid dreams because my world was crackling with the brilliant color of the paint I used so often in my artwork. Jumping out of bed to open the window, I could smell that something was terribly wrong. The entire apartment complex behind our house was on fire! I was about to wake my brothers, who were surprisingly still asleep, when I heard my father screaming: "Boys, get out of bed and run! Run outside! The building behind us is on fire, and the wind is blowing it our way!"

We stood in the street in our pajamas, while Dad kept us very close to him. Not long after, my mother came bolting up the street from the pizza shop. When she saw us, her relief that we'd survived was palpable, but her next emotion was clearly grief over the loss of our home. By this time, the fire had snaked around to our block, and the blazing buildings were falling like dominos.

That sad night, the fire consumed most of our street, but it somehow skipped our house. It was easy to see that my parents were in shock, but they finally chalked it up to one of those "lucky breaks" in life. I didn't believe it was that simple, for I knew that a force far greater than the fire was protecting us. I tried looking for answers or signs in my books, but I couldn't find out why this had happened. All I could do was be thankful that the little we had was still ours.

Life quickly returned to normal—including the winter weather, which brought its typical sub-zero temperatures. On those chilly mornings, my mother would be the first up; I'd hear her and wait under the sheets until I could smell the mouth-watering doughnuts baking in the old gas oven.

For my mother, this served a dual purpose. Not only would she have some fresh breakfast for us, but she could also open the oven door to help heat the kitchen before our tiny feet hit the cold linoleum. You see, there usually wasn't enough money for oil to heat our apartment. Still, I'd get out of bed and nearly freeze as I ran to the kitchen. "Purple. Just five," I'd blurt out, announcing the color she wanted to wear and the number of dollars in her purse.

"How'd you know?" she'd respond.

My father would be gone by then because he got up at the crack of dawn, which, frankly, was a relief. When he returned at night, I'd keep a mental note of how much amber liquid was in the bottle when the evening started. If the bottle was empty and in the trash bin by the time I went to bed, then I knew that a day that started so pleasantly with the baked doughnuts would end with potential ugliness. During Dad's drinking bouts, his behavior would be unpredictable at best.

Soon I would find that "others" were helping me cope with the sad facts of my day-to-day existence. In fact, they would save my young life.

Take, for example, what happened to me when I was ten. Dorchester had its fair share of beautiful old trees, and even though I wasn't an athletic kid, I had a favorite maple I loved to climb. I'd go up as high as possible and stare out at the world from this lofty perch, which was three stories high—a place where no one could touch me.

One day, I was nestled about halfway up the tree when I heard a "crrrrraaaacking" sound, and I realized that the branch holding me up was breaking. With a loud snap, the thick piece of weathered wood gave way, and I began to plummet toward the ground at an alarming speed. An image of me lying in a hospital bed with multiple broken bones flashed before my eyes, but something was preventing that from happening.

I realized that I wasn't really falling that fast at all—my arms and legs weren't flailing, and I didn't even think to scream. I was being handled with extreme care, descending as if in slow motion, with my eyes open the entire time. In fact, I'd come as close to flying as a human being could imagine . . . and I landed softly on my back without a scratch. Someone, something, some *miracle* had carried me down to safety.

No, I didn't fall—I was placed back on the earth with the broken tree branch in my hand like a souvenir from my trip to this Spirit Amusement Park. What a ride!

It was only the beginning of even stranger things interrupting my daily existence, in much bigger ways than before. A few weeks after the tree incident, I was running down the street with plans to visit the home of this new kid on our block. I sprinted up the triple-decker building's stone stairs, and I could see that the front door was wide open, so luckily I could just dash into the hallway without being buzzed inside. I started to enter the vestibule, but I found myself knocked back on my butt as if I'd hit a wall. Something stopped me from going into that building. Slowly, I stood up and reached out with my hand to see if there was some sort of invisible force field, similar to the type that Captain Kirk from *Star Trek* might stumble upon in one of his adventures. There was nothing there.

Looking back, I realized that I was prevented from going into that building for a reason. Either I was being stopped from hurting myself at that exact moment, or I bumped into "something" or "someone" on their way out of the building. Whatever it was, I was sure most people couldn't see or feel it—well, most *living* people, anyway.

chapter 3

CALIFORNIA

"LOOK AT THE NEW KID—WHAT'S UP with him? He's so quiet and freaky." That's what I routinely heard as a teenager. I tried my best to ignore the taunts.

By the time I entered high school, I'd thrown in the towel when it came to the teenage popularity game. My family had moved from Dorchester to a smaller town, so I was dubbed "the city boy" or "that weird quiet kid." I hardly ever used my abilities while I was a teenager because I was afraid of those horrible names the kids called people who were really different (the teasing I already got was bad enough). So I pushed away my fascination with the metaphysical and suppressed my special talent in an attempt to be a normal teenager.

As it turned out, I only got close to a few of my classmates because most of them were obsessed with sports, dating, and College Board exams. I didn't care about any of the above, which meant that I was never part of the groups that gathered for lunch in the cafeteria. You'd usually find me sitting apart with my nose in a book (again).

Every once in a while, my few friends would say, "Go ahead, John. Do that thing you do." But I didn't do it often.

After I graduated from high school, I sought out a real purpose in life. I did find something that featured being surrounded by white light—but it's not what you think. I met a young woman named Cathy who was setting up a new business as a commercial photographer in Boston. I worked part time as her assistant, and I loved being in her cavernous studio, watching the dazzling white flashes going off in my eyes.

Cathy promoted me to studio manager and taught me all about the art of photography. She also took it upon herself to teach me some etiquette, helping me smooth out some of my rough Dorchester edges. When those lessons were complete, she brought me to some of the social gatherings around Boston. Watching her relaxed, confident manner as she chatted with people gave me the courage to overcome my shyness.

On the day I turned 21, Cathy surprised me with a wonderful gift. "John, I bought us two tickets to go to California," she said. "I'm going to show my portfolio to some record companies. I'll also be doing a shoot, so I'll need your help."

I think I'd packed my few things into my ancient suitcase in about three seconds because I was afraid that she'd certainly change her mind about taking me with her, and I didn't want to risk missing the trip of a lifetime.

◎

As Cathy and I cruised some 30,000 feet over the Rocky Mountains. I felt my own spirit soaring with the possibilities that awaited me. I was flying, and I don't just mean physically.

Everything I knew about California came from movie magazines, books, and television. I imagined that when we arrived, we'd be surrounded by Hollywood movie stars, bright lights, beaches, and nonstop sunshine . . . well, I was right about one of them.

Cathy had to make her rounds to various music companies, so she dropped me off at the beach to relax. As sand scratched my toes, I waded out into the ocean until the waves caught me in their trap. I quickly learned how to bodysurf, and it was vastly different from splashing around that fire hydrant in my old neighborhood. The freedom of the Pacific Ocean made my heart soar.

I went to Venice Beach to watch the street performers, artists, roller skaters, and, yes, sidewalk psychics. "Do you know what a tarot card is, young man?" asked one of them. Did I know? I could talk tarot for two days with this woman.

One night Cathy and I drove down Hollywood Boulevard with the top down on our rental car and the warm, soothing Santa Ana winds tousling our hair. Then we went to the beach and strolled along the Santa Monica pier, checking out its giant Ferris wheel and the street vendors who peddled everything from fake tattoos to huge clouds of cotton candy. I felt as if I were living an entire "do over" childhood in those few days, and I realized how much I'd missed as a boy.

While we were gazing at the sunset, my eyes fixated on the thousands of tiny lights dancing on the water as the sun disappeared over the horizon. In my mind, I decided that the lights were so free that they were simply jumping for joy. I knew that the energy of the ocean's water could be both powerful and healing, and I felt a wonderful sense of inner peace being there. It was as though my shackles had been released.

I knew I'd be back.

Of course, money (or should I say, the lack of it) was the perpetual problem. I couldn't afford to live my dream . . . at least not yet. Back home in Boston, with a renewed enthusiasm and purpose, I went to work full time for a hotel, and there I met a woman who became one of my best friends. Joyce was actually my boss, but during the lulls in hotel activity, we'd talk about our hopes and dreams for the future. I told her about my plans to move to California.

"I've always had a secret wish to move there myself," she said. And, without much more discussion, we smiled at each other, knowing what we needed to do.

My goal wouldn't come cheaply, so I spent every spare moment working, planning, and saving my cash for my "California-Here-I-Come Fund." As the months wore on, I was really proud of myself because I knew I was never going to have to say I "someday," "maybe," "could have," "would have," or "should have" done something. I truly believe that you're only in this body once, and every day is a new opportunity and a fresh start. So many people quash their dreams based on their fears of failure—they "play it safe" and stay where they are in their lives, never moving on or fulfilling their true potential. People believe risk is unsafe; I believe that playing it safe is the ultimate risk.

It just felt right to go to California, even though I had no idea where I'd live or what I'd do once I got there. Destiny, however, intervened, and I received a call from an old friend who was actually living in Los Angeles. She said that Joyce and I could stay with her for a little while, and I said a silent prayer of thanks. It isn't strange at all when the universe intervenes and just places the solution right in your lap.

◎

Bittersweet is the only word that can really describe what it was like to leave my family. Even though I was in my 20s, it was still the first time that I'd be far away from home. I clutched my siblings close to me, embracing them as if I were going away forever. Even my father gave me a quick hug and said through a choked voice, "You should go."

The hardest thing was looking into my mother's proud but pained face. She clung; I clung. She cried; I cried. She wouldn't remove her arms from me—my father finally had to peel back her thin fingers, one by one, so I could pull myself out of her grasp.

I loved California even more the second time around. I couldn't get enough of the weather, the beaches, and the people. Soon I discovered that my new home was blessed with dozens of metaphysical bookstores and psychics working openly and professionally across the city. I even heard of a woman who made a living channeling dolphins—I'd seen it all!

Once I was settled, I felt that all-too-familiar nagging sensation to look inward. One day I saw a flyer that advertised meditation groups, so I called the number and signed up. Again, it was feeding time for my passion for the unexplained.

A few months later, I found a radio station that featured a psychic from Southern California named Vincent J. Barra. His specialty was giving readings on the air to help people work out their issues. I listened to him religiously each week, and learned that Vincent had been doing psychic work for more than 25 years and was well known in the business. He was also a master of Reiki (pronounced *ray-kee*), an ancient Tibetan healing method.

I signed up for Vincent's lectures and sat there spellbound week after week. Often at the end of the evening, kind of like an encore, Vincent would give psychic readings to members of the audience. This was the first time I'd seen this sort of thing in person. And even though the chairs in the hall were uncomfortable, I didn't move an inch while he gave spot readings, moving from one person to another. Vincent was down to earth and just called it like he saw it.

"You were very close with your grandmother, who also saw what you see," Vincent whispered to me during one of his presentations. He didn't have to ask if he was right—my response was written all over my face.

I'd always leave those lectures feeling a little giddy, because watching him demonstrate psychic ability, as opposed to my reading about it in a book, was incredibly satisfying. Gathering my courage after five lectures, I finally approached him and introduced myself. We soon became friends, and he was one of the first people willing to listen to my story. The first time I told him about my childhood experiences, it was such a relief. It was like taking that first gulp of air after holding my breath for two decades.

Vincent and I would sometimes talk until three in the morning, and he helped me understand that every psychic needs a good mentor. It's always wonderful to find someone who knows exactly what you're going through and doesn't pass judgment. There's also a famous saying that promises, "When the student is ready, the teacher will come." Vincent was that teacher for me when I was in my early 20s, and he remains a mentor and good friend to this day.

◎

A few years passed while I bounced around doing odd jobs and enjoying L.A.'s nightlife. It's so easy to get caught up in that city's pace, running from one place to another, working and socializing. But the long hours started to take their toll, and eventually I found that I had little time for spiritual endeavors. My life was clearly spinning out of control.

At the time, Joyce was working for a major hotel in the L.A. area. One day she called to ask if I'd like to be a bartender there for a little while. I said it was perfect timing and an opportunity to work different hours, which would also offer me some personal time. Soon I was mixing drinks for the Beverly Hills elite, who used the hotel for weddings, premieres, and all sorts of group events. It was a busy job, but it was good to work with Joyce again.

I settled into the routine and started to organize my life. Things seemed to be getting back on track. Little did I know that my life was about to change in a most dramatic way.

chapter 4

THE SWITCH GETS TURNED ON

THERE'S SOMETHING ALMOST peaceful about Los Angeles in the middle of the night. The smog often evaporates and is replaced by a jet-black sky—and if you look hard enough, it seems like the stars are dancing over the mountains.

The night I almost died, the meteorologist said that it was supposed to be just such a night. I was finishing a long and tedious evening pouring drinks for a wedding reception. Although it was good money and I enjoyed serving elegantly clad hotel guests a glass of bubbly to toast a couple's new beginning, once the festivities wore on, the guests usually drank too much and their party manners often disappeared.

This particular night was worse than ever because a few of my co-workers were sick, which left me on my feet for close to eight hours straight. As the party wound down, I finally took a short break and gazed out the window. The heavens chose to open at that exact moment, and the gardens were suddenly running with torrents of water, flooding the parched ground.

I looked at Joyce, and we both shook our heads. "Perfect. Just our luck," I muttered.

An hour later, I was running across the parking lot, fumbling with my keys, and getting soaked at the same time. I shook my head again.

Let me just say that those who live in L.A. aren't used to hazardous driving conditions. But the Massachusetts native in me knew to take it slow as I drove out of the parking lot, because the once-dry pavement was now wet and slippery. In fact, it was almost like driving on the icy winter streets back home.

A few blocks later, I wasn't thinking about the conditions anymore. I was exhausted and hungry, and my feet were throbbing—I just wanted to get home and crawl into bed. However, my drive home was going to take even longer with the rain, which was absolutely pouring down now. I couldn't even see anything through my windshield except my trusty wipers struggling to do their job.

Everything happened in a split second, as accidents so often do. All of a sudden, my car was bouncing off the guardrails and hydroplaning because my wheels hit a big pool of water and lifted off the road. I glanced quickly to the left, praying that I wouldn't slide off the concrete and down a steep incline. In a moment of horror, I knew my fate. I was going to die.

I closed my eyes.

At that moment, I felt something take control of the car, rip it back from the edge, and set it onto the road again. But I wasn't safe—not by a long shot. The conditions were far too dangerous and slippery for the car to simply stop, and my still out-of-control vehicle began to slide precariously to the edge again. Even though I held off the temptation to jam on the brakes, the car spun around several times in tight circles before finally skidding diagonally across the road. Again, a strong force began to slow me down on this (thankfully) deserted freeway.

As the car started to come to a stop, I opened my eyes and was instantly blinded by a flash of pure white light, which darted inside the car. One minute it was there, the next it was gone. The light needed no explanation. It was just like the one I'd experienced that night in my bedroom when I was a boy.

I couldn't wrap my mind around what was happening or think about the deeper meaning, for the first order of business was my own physical safety. My car was badly damaged, yet it was still running, so both of us limped home. In the darkness of my bedroom, I tried to sleep, but my mind was in overdrive. I kept thinking about the accident, playing the scene over and over in my head. One thing was clear: Certain events are fated to happen. When you have a trauma in your life, like my accident, it can change you and your outlook on life forever.

This was a major wake-up call for me. Frankly, one of these calls was enough. Good thing I realized this back then or I might be speaking to you through another *medium* right now (hey, it always helps to have a sense of humor).

I used my car crash as an opportunity to get my life back on the path that was mapped out for me as a child. My route was preplanned; it was in my head and my heart. I just needed to believe and trust.

After the accident, a strange thing happened to me. I could feel strong and consistent energy coursing through my system, as if a gentle current was continually running up and down my body. It felt as if I'd been connected to some new power supply, but I couldn't describe it or explain it beyond the fact that it was a thrilling sensation.

Over and over I thought about the light I saw on the road at the exact moment of the accident. Was it protecting me? (Now, of course, I understand exactly what happened to me on that road. My energy system [better known as *chakras*] was opening up and starting to operate at full force for the first time. It was as if all the barriers and blockades that had been set up for me had been broken down.)

Back then, I felt the need to tell people about the transformation going on inside me, and I telephoned several of my friends. But those calls weren't about me at all—they were about *them*. Something within me had been switched on. What was once pushed away was back with full force.

Those first few calls were intense because I could feel and see things about my friends' lives even though we weren't face-to-face, things that I couldn't have possibly known. To put it bluntly, I saw their pasts and their potential futures.

I'd rattle things off without even thinking. For example, one of my friends called to see how I was after the accident, and the first thing I blurted out was, "Margo, did you have fun at the zoo yesterday? Why did you call Rick when you said you'd never speak to him again?"

She was caught a bit off guard, so I launched into my next question. "Who is this new guy you met with the scar on his upper lip?"

Margo answered with a little confusion. "John, I did go to the zoo, and Rick needed my help with his daughter. But

I don't know anyone who has a scar on his lip. I don't know who you're talking about. What's going on?"

"I'm talking about Sam," I said matter-of-factly.

About 48 hours later, Margo called me back. "John, you're not going to believe this, but I met a new guy named Sam last night, and he has a scar just like you mentioned. He fell off his bike as a kid." She paused. *"What in the world is going on with you?"*

What was going on with me was anyone's guess. It was almost as if I were standing in other people's physical spaces and in their lives. I knew so much . . . sometimes too much. It was an exhilarating feeling that left me excited, a little scared, and nervous all at the same time. I even tried to describe it to my friends. "It's like that heady feeling you get when you're at the top of a roller coaster and you know in one second that you're about to feel the biggest rush," I'd say, but the blank looks on their faces told me that they didn't understand. I couldn't blame them.

I had to figure out a way to harness this energy or gift so that I could live my own life. So, for the first time in years, I looked up some of my old, trusted friends—my dusty books. I found some of the answers I sought in biographies of legendary mediums and psychics including Eileen Garrett, Gerard Croiset, Peter Hurkos, Arthur Ford, and many more. It comforted me to see how those who paved the way learned how to harness their abilities and manage their own demanding lives instead of letting their lives run them.

As I read, I discovered that I could actually open and tune down my psychic abilities. Ah, that's what I needed—a shut-off valve. I knew at this point that I was definitely psychic, and I'd embrace that fact even more when I figured out how to turn it down.

My studies fascinated and frightened me because I was rapidly going down a road where it was impossible to do a U-turn, and I wasn't sure if I wanted this life. Would I just be known as a freak again? But unlike my childhood, this time I simply couldn't push my psychic abilities away or hide them because they were hitting me faster and harder then ever as each day passed. I could feel myself developing, getting stronger and more confident. It was much like the way an athlete progresses after each training session.

Unlike how it was during my childhood, I couldn't sit in my bedroom and just read. I still had to pay the bills, which is why I continued to work at the hotel. Somehow I found the courage to walk up to fellow employees and ask them if I could give them a reading or tell them something about themselves. I figured that if I could, it would help release the energy that was constantly building up inside of me.

Like anyone starting out, I was learning while I was doing, so there were times when I got it right . . . and there were many times when I didn't. And I experienced a lot of comical moments as well, such as when I'd walk up to someone and simply ask how they were, and they'd gaze at me in horror and scream, "Why?!"

One executive, who was a regular guest and had obviously heard something about me, said, "Don't even look at me." I certainly didn't have the power to see into her soul—what I *was* doing was being friendly, polite, and businesslike because it seemed rude to look away. And some of the more religious people in the hotel would bless themselves with the sign of the cross when I walked by them.

These responses—call it feedback—were quite fascinating. I realized that most people don't actually know how psychic abilities work, so their fear is born mainly from ignorance and a lack of understanding. There were many times when I was confused myself about the information I received. But I really wondered what I should do with it. Should I even deliver it at all?

For instance, I knew that my supervisor's wife, who was expecting a baby, was about to have a few complications because her uterus was tilted. I didn't even know what a tilted uterus was or if it was serious. I finally plucked up the courage and found the right words to talk to her husband without causing undue alarm. Thankfully, he wasn't offended—he was actually grateful. It turned out that his wife did have a few rough moments during birth because of her tilted uterus. Everything turned out fine, but I was never worried—I *knew* it would be fine.

Next I tried my hand on the patrons who sat at the bar. A customer would walk up and I'd say, "This one's on the house for your birthday."

They'd do a double-take. "How could you know it's my birthday? It's not like you carded me."

Laughing it off, I'd say, "Oh, you just had that birthday look."

There were times when I'd see different symbols in my mind's eye. Mini-movies played out right above or behind my customers, but they were playing on an invisible screen that only I could see. For instance, an elderly gentleman walked up to the bar one day, and I saw a map of Europe behind his head. "So, you're going overseas," I said, as though I were making small talk while I mixed his gin and tonic.

"I just got back," he replied, with a somewhat quizzical look on his face.

A stylish woman in her 60s ordered a martini, and as she was waiting, I decided to raise the stakes and go for it. "So, you're divorced now and have four children. One of them is coming to visit next week."

She looked at me dumbfounded. "He's coming from New York," she said.

This went on and on.

As you can imagine, some people looked at me and laughed, while others walked away freaked out. Some would indulge me and ask me to tell them more, which occasionally resulted in a larger tip! Nowadays, I advise people who believe that they have special abilities to *never* walk up to a stranger and start giving them information like this. To put it bluntly, I was untrained and inexperienced, and I'm sure I came across as downright rude at times. There's an ethical responsibility when you do this work, but at the time, what did I know about ethics? I was basically in psychic kindergarten.

Naturally, word got out around Los Angeles, a city where what and who is "hot" changes on a daily basis. Customers were soon coming to sit on my barstools, but not to quench their thirsts. They'd heard about the "psychic barman," and they were thirsty to know if I could "see" something about them. And in my naiveté, I aimed to please.

"Your wife is angry with you—why don't you bring her some of her favorite tulips? You know, the pink ones," I'd say.

"You have a baby on the way," I said to a nice girl in tweed.

To another, I whispered, "Don't worry about the guy you just broke up with. He's still getting over his last relationship. You'll meet Mr. Perfect in a month, and he'll definitely be ready for a new relationship."

To a sullen middle-aged man, I said, "Oh, cheer up. You'll find another job quickly, where your skills will be better used and recognized. But I agree—it wasn't fair that they fired you today."

A few people greeted my "news flashes" with a hostility that surprised me. "Keep it to yourself!" they'd say. I could only shrug and keep pushing on, pouring beverages and serving up the information to anyone who would listen. Finally, I must have gone over the top with it because I was advised by management to take psychic readings off the menu immediately—or else.

Meanwhile, Margo and a few of my other friends were encouraging me do readings on the side and in a more professional manner. My answer was a simple and loud "No way!" I wasn't ready to put myself out in front of people who hoped that I could sort out their lives. I could imagine that look of naked hope in their eyes as they sat there. What if I didn't have any answers? What if I let them down? I couldn't take that sort of disappointment, and I could only imagine what it would do to them. The responsibility of it all was overwhelming. Why go through that sort of torture?

Finally, I gave into the pressure, realizing that I could do a few readings over the phone, and that way I wouldn't have to see the person's face. I actually worked this way for a few months, and it was fine until Margo called one day.

"John, I have a friend who needs a reading, and she wants to sit with you," she begged.

We did a little dance for a week. She persisted, and I declined. She pushed, and I pushed back. She nagged until I finally gave in. That's how I gave my first "official" in-person reading (or "sitting," as we psychics call it).

As the appointed time drew near, I paced up and down the already worn carpet, smoking cigarettes in rapid succession. *What am I thinking?* I kept asking myself. *What am I doing? Can I do this? Will she laugh? Or walk out?*

Then came the knock. I took a long, deep breath and opened the door.

— ◎ —

chapter 5

THE QUICKENING

SUE WAS A TALL, BEAUTIFUL woman in her mid-20s, with a smart cropped haircut. I saw Margo walk in behind her for the necessary introductions, and sighed with relief when it became clear that she'd be staying for the reading, too.

I lit incense and told the women how I'd meditated for half an hour, surrounding myself with white light—something I still do before I see clients. Although I think creating a calm and relaxed atmosphere for readings is necessary, justifying what I did and why I did it isn't. But I was worried that Margo and Sue could hear my heart thumping through my chest or see my hands shaking.

"Why don't we sit down," I said, taking a deep breath because I was anxious to start. "Sue, I'd like to hold something of yours, like a ring or a watch. It should be something that's always belonged to you." I'd read that this practice, called *psychometry,* would help me tune in to a client's energy.

Sue handed me a beautiful aquamarine ring with a gold band. I took it in my hand and immediately felt the energy in my body speed ahead. Yet I still wondered if I'd pick up anything: *Would there be a connection?*

It turns out that I needn't have worried—images suddenly flooded my mind, and their meanings began to take form. Words formed on their own, and they just flowed out of my mouth without any editing from me whatsoever. Suddenly, I began rattling off facts about Sue's life. "You work in the medical profession, and you're still going to school," I stated. She confirmed that she was studying to be a psychologist.

My heart soared because this was going in the right direction. I continued, "Isn't it true that you had a few medical problems when you were younger? In fact, you were very sick."

I noticed Sue's eyes welling up with tears, but the words kept pouring out of me. "It's a miracle that you're still here, isn't it?" I quietly asked her as a teardrop fell down her cheek.

Margo's presence in the room faded. My focus was totally on Sue. It was as if the two of us were the only two people in the universe—our auras had blended together, and everything else became superfluous at that moment in time. I started to see a plan in her life: how she got to where she was, the obstacles in front of her, and how she could maneuver herself around some of them. Sue's life was being revealed to me like the pages of a book.

Like so many of us, she wanted to know about her love life, while I was more focused on where her academic life was taking her. "Let me be honest, Sue," I said. "Right now, your career is the most important thing in your life. But romance will happen after you take care of your career." Then a line popped into my mind that I'd use many times over the next few years: "There cannot be a 'we' until there is a 'me.'"

She nodded as if she totally understood what this meant.

An hour passed, and I was still talking while Sue took detailed notes—as if every word would later be studied, repeated, and memorized. I felt the energy and the images begin to fade, as though someone was turning the volume down. I wondered if what I'd told her was enough. My answer came when I looked up at my client, who was smiling broadly. She looked content, but *I* was filled with questions: *Is the information correct? Was it what she expected? Did it make sense to her?*

"John, this reading was very healing for me. I just want you to know that you confirmed many things that I've wondered about for a long time," Sue said, standing to shake my sweaty hand.

A short time after she departed (with Margo beaming widely at me), I collapsed on the couch, emotionally drained. Yet part of me was actually restless, as though my body was still charged up. You see, I was my own worst critic back then. I felt I needed to know everything about a client. Now I know that the information I get is what I'm supposed to get and give out. I simply try to interpret it to the best of my ability and pass it on.

Margo wasn't surprised that my first reading was such a success, but she gave me a couple of days before she called to taunt me in her good-natured way. "I told you so," she said, laughing. She also wasn't shocked when I was suddenly too busy to hang out with her.

"Sorry, but I have another phone reading today," I said, ignoring how tired I'd become. Working full time at the hotel was still necessary to pay the bills; the readings were something I just did on the side.

"John, why don't you just do readings and quit your day job?" my friends started to ask me.

"I'm not ready for that yet," I'd say.

But when I was asked to do readings at a popular L.A. aromatherapy shop, I knew that I couldn't avoid or run away from the work anymore. Sitting in the middle of the store, I'd read for the customers with my recently purchased deck of tarot cards, which were more of a prop for me, as I rarely needed them once I got going. (But it was nice to have something to do with my hands.) It felt great to give out information, because with each reading, it was like putting a pin in an overinflated balloon. The energy that built up in my system would actually seep out, which was a great relief.

As I continued to give readings, one problem remained: There was no one I could turn to for professional advice on the subject. I was basically on my own, except for some words of wisdom from my friend Vincent, who had a strong belief that it was better to let me figure things out for myself rather than use him as a crutch. "The best way to learn is to just do it," he told me repeatedly.

So here I was, just doing it. Deep down, I had a sneaking suspicion that Vincent had helped me as much as he could, and now it was up to me to find my own answers. I decided to allow others who had their own special abilities give me a little advice. What could it hurt?

Luckily, there was a tarot card reader on staff at the aromatherapy shop. One night when neither of us was working, I asked her to do a reading for me, and she readily agreed. A few minutes into our session, she looked in my eyes and said, "John, you're going to be very well known, and you're going to come out with a book someday."

I shook my head and said, "Are you on medication or what?"

I was only just getting started, and she was telling me that I'd be famous? *A book!* Uh-huh. I just tucked that information in the back of my mind and went on with my not-so-famous life.

Even though I wasn't allowed to do readings at the hotel anymore, I was doing more and more of them at my apartment. My clients were telling their friends and word was spreading, which was the best compliment I could receive. (I always recommend that you choose a reputable psychic or medium by word of mouth. Find someone who has gone to one, and ask if the experience was helpful and worthwhile.)

It became apparent that some external force was monitoring my schedule so I didn't burn out. For instance, when the bartending work slowed down, my phone would ring off the hook for readings, and when the readings slowed down, the bartending picked up. It was as if there was some universally controlled balancing act going on.

The next two years passed in the blink of an eye. I built up quite a client list in the Los Angeles area, but I still wasn't totally content because my mind remained in overdrive. I wasn't really sure if I wanted to make this my life's mission. As long as I worked during the day, the psychic work was like a fascinating second job. Somehow, I knew that I'd have to make a decision between the two.

It helped to immerse myself in the psychic arts. A popular new hangout for me was West Hollywood's Bodhi Tree Bookstore, and it became my home away from home. I'd sit there for hours . . . luckily no one ever threw out the guy who treated the place like his own personal study. In my spare time, I went to every metaphysical event on the calendar, driving from one side of the city to the other. At one such expo, I met an interesting woman named Adrian, who was fun to talk to about spiritual subjects and life.

"You know, I'm a psychic, and I do readings on the side," I told her as we exchanged phone numbers and said our good-byes. I thought that would be the end of it.

To my surprise, I received a call from her the very next day, saying that a friend of hers really needed to see me. So I set an appointment and decided that I'd go to Adrian's house and read for Maury, a cute, petite woman with deep brown eyes. The minute we met, I could tell by her light Southern drawl that she was born and raised in Mississippi. You didn't need to be a psychic to figure that one out.

As I started to read for Maury, I noticed vivid colors building up around her. This always means that the client has some artistic or creative ability. Maury confirmed that she studied interior design, and I went on to present her with other facts. I described in detail a current school project she was working on that still needed finishing, and she nodded in agreement. Smiling, I was about to go on with the reading when something very different began to happen. In fact, it was so sudden and unexpected that it shocked both of us.

One minute, we were talking about her design career, and the next I felt as if something had shifted in the room—and it had. Now I refer to this shift as "the quickening." Basically, this meant that Maury and I weren't alone anymore . . . not by a long shot.

I noticed that sitting right beside Maury was an elderly woman with a lovely, warm smile. Knowing I couldn't keep this quiet, I said, "Maury, there's an older woman sitting beside you, and there's something strange about her clothes— none of the colors match. And I think she's talking about a diamond."

Yes, now I could hear this older woman's voice in my own head, and she kept saying the same thing over and over again: "She'll know who I am. Mention the diamond! Mention the diamond!" Of course, I did exactly what she asked.

Soon I was talking so fast that I didn't even stop to check in with Maury and notice her reaction. I didn't have to wait long, though, because she loudly gasped for air and started to cry. I came over to console her, and I finally asked, "Who *is* the woman?"

In a broken voice, she said, "John, it's my Great Aunt Ada, who raised me. She was color blind, yet she insisted on choosing her own clothes. Our family never knew what she'd show up wearing."

It turns out that Maury and Ada had a very strong bond, right up to her death ten years earlier. "She loved me and was always so kind to me. I could always count on her. Even though she's gone, I have something to remind me of her. I inherited her diamond ring." Maury sobbed, "I miss her so much."

When she composed herself, we sat down again and I suggested that we continue our journey together. "Is she still there?" Maury whispered.

"Yes, she's here," I said. "She's smiling, and she said to tell you that she's always close."

After this extraordinary reading, I once again collapsed on the couch. I couldn't believe what had happened. "Great. First, I have to accept that I'm a psychic with all that goes with that responsibility. Now I'm talking to the dead!" I said to myself.

◎

There's a big difference between being a psychic and being a medium. A psychic can pick up things, be they images or feelings from their surroundings, and they can read people's auras. Mediums pick up the images, thoughts, and feelings from those who have "passed on." A medium should get a link to ensure that they're working on a mediumship level and not psychically. All mediums are psychic, but not all psychics are mediums.

I had a sneaking suspicion why I was suddenly communicating with spirits who had departed this physical world. After doing two years of steady psychic readings, I must have reached an entirely new level of ability. Not only was I *seeing* these spirits, but they were also *communicating* directly with me, or should I say *through* me.

Something equally odd happened with that early reading. I found out later that Maury couldn't wait to play the cassette tape of our session, and when I spoke about her design career, my voice sounded perfectly normal on the tape. But when Great Aunt Ada appeared to "do her thing," the tape sped up to the point where everything sounded like it was on hyperspeed. When Ada's energy faded and she was gone, our voices returned to normal on the tape. Somehow the spirit world was jump-starting the entire atmosphere.

This marked the first time that *they* were present during a conversation. From that point on, they showed up at every sitting I conducted.

A few days later, Adrian decided that she wanted a reading with me herself. As usual, I began our session by asking to hold something that belonged to her. Adrian handed me her favorite gold band, which instantly caused an array of images to flood in. I began to tell her about the year ahead, and she interrupted to ask me some specific questions about her career, finances, and of course, love life. It turned out that she was very interested in a special guy who had been playing on her heart for a very long time. I was starting to give her some advice when . . . it happened again. My senses seemed to click into gear, and everything accelerated. In other words, I had another quickening.

I was halfway through talking about the love interest when I just changed tracks and said, "Adrian, has your father passed away?"

The shock registered on her face. "Yes," she said in a pained voice. "It happened about six months ago."

I felt her dad so strongly at that precise moment that I had to ask, "Does the name Ken mean anything to you?"

"Yes, yes," she cried. "That was his name!" Adrian sobbed as she told me how her dad passed away in her arms. "He was very sick, and his body started to shut down right in front of me. I felt his spirit slowly slip away, and I held him until he wasn't here anymore."

When she composed herself, Adrian had questions. "I need to know two things. Where is my father now? And is he okay?'"

As she asked these things, I could feel Ken's unconditional love for his daughter. And then I started seeing images of bookcases. "Did he have a bookcase, Adrian?" I asked, which was a silly question because next I said, "He had tons of books, correct?"

"Yes," she gasped. "My dad was a big reader, and he especially loved books on Eastern spirituality and philosophy. He was way ahead of his time."

In my mind's eye, I saw Ken's bookcase and found myself being directed to one particular book on the shelf. "Your father wants you to go to his bookcase," I told her. "On the second shelf from the top, you'll find an old brown book. It's the fourth one from the left. He wants you to look inside that book, for there will be something there to answer both of your questions.

"He's very specific, Adrian." I continued. "He wants me to make sure that you look at that specific book," I told her. After I finished that sentence, her father was gone. I tried to continue with the psychic reading, but there was no way I could shift my own energy back into a lower gear.

Meanwhile, Adrian was so filled with emotion that it actually took her a few days to find the courage to approach her father's bookcase. She tried to prepare herself emotionally, but there was nothing else she could do but work on blind faith. Without any problem, she found the exact book that her father described to me, and inside was a special message on a yellowed piece of paper. Adrian lovingly pulled out a poem titled "Soar Into the Cosmic Blue," which she thought her father had written some 20 years earlier. The words seemed to answer all of Adrian's questions about her father's whereabouts and whether he was okay, for it ended with a line that described what it felt like "to fly to the rim of heaven."

Ken's love for his daughter was so strong that he had to show her that he had, in fact, reached the rim of heaven, and that he was content, pain free, and happy. I wonder if he'd known the true message when he wrote that poem so many years ago, or if he had any inkling that someday it would be a final message for his daughter. Needless to say, this was a very special reading for me.

After the experience with Adrian, my fascination and interest was so intense that I threw myself into researching mediumship. I wanted to be more in control—I didn't want to just let the quickenings happen, I wanted to be ready for them.

Books on Spiritualism helped. Spiritualism is a belief system that's based on the continuity of life and communication with Spirit, through the spiritual gift of mediumship. It's also a religion, a philosophy, and for so many, a way of life. Although Spiritualism was actually founded in 1848 in

America, it flourished in England. There are still Spiritualist churches in the U.S., but not nearly as many as there are "across the pond," as they say. Mediumship not only caught the attention of the British people, but scholars there have never given up their quest to learn as much as they can about this fascinating subject.

The Spiritualists' faith has a very calming and healing effect on its believers because they're taught that we don't die, and loved ones who have passed are still alive and well in Spirit. Too many Hollywood movies have portrayed this faith in a spooky light and have given us the wrong impression about what Spiritualism is today.

I knew that if I was going to develop my abilities even further, I'd need some hands-on experience courtesy of people far more knowledgeable than those I could find in Los Angeles. But who would help me?

chapter 6

LEARNING TO TRUST

SOMETIMES YOU HAVE TO LET GO of the river's edge to see where the flow takes you. In other words, you must surrender to fate. . . .

I couldn't believe that I was now 34 years old—more than ten years had passed since I'd first arrived in California. As that decade grew to a close, I was headed for unemployment because the hotel where I worked was up for sale. It was obvious that the new owners would be looking to make their own changes, both in operations *and* staff. Once again, I was in limbo. I knew that I was comfortable and secure living in L.A., and working at the hotel meshed well with doing readings on the side.

One night I walked through the hotel after my shift was over. Questions about what to do with my life filled my head, and I was so distracted that I managed to step on some guy's foot. Since it seemed as if he'd appeared from nowhere, the poor guy got my full body weight, and we both jumped in surprise.

Luckily, he didn't yelp in pain (although no one would have blamed him). However, I was mortified when I stepped on him, thinking for certain that I'd broken his toes. "I'm so sorry! That was very careless of me," I said.

In a smooth English accent, he brushed off the entire incident as if it were nothing.

"You don't sound like you're from here," I said. As soon as I uttered the words, I realized how stupid and banal they sounded. Nevertheless, he was still being cordial and friendly toward me, and although I'd never seen him before in my life, I felt as though there was something familiar about him. The man went on to explain that he was visiting from England, and as he mentioned his country, my body froze for a split second.

Little did this fellow know that my kitchen table was covered with books from English mediums and Spiritualist magazines from all over the United Kingdom. We introduced ourselves, and before I knew it, Simon and I had found chairs in the lobby. As we chatted, I think he could tell that I was harmless (except for the damage I'd done to his toes) and fascinated with his homeland, so he told me about England, and so much of the history that went with it. He painted a verbal picture of the Balloon Fiesta in Bristol, his hometown, where hundreds of hot-air balloons of all shapes and sizes filled the skies. At night, the balloons were illuminated, setting the sky on fire with thousands of colors. I was enchanted by his descriptions.

"I have an old Victorian house overlooking the harbor," Simon told me, "and I rent out the top floor if you or any of your friends ever think of visiting Bristol."

This was too much to take in at once. He was offering a room to a complete stranger who nearly put him in a cast? Just talking to Simon sealed the deal. I felt that destiny wasn't just *calling*—this time it came with a view. Now my mind was *really* racing with questions.

Two months later, my answers came. The hotel was sold, and I was laid off. I had no reason to stay in California. The door was open.

Going to England was a spur-of-the-moment decision funded by the meager savings in my bank account. It was also supported by my friends, who repeatedly told me to get out of L.A. and take this opportunity of a lifetime. In fact, they literally pushed me onto the plane before I had a chance to think about what I was doing. They all knew me so well—if I'd stopped to think, I might very well have changed my mind.

Soon I was halfway over the Atlantic and far away from the sparkling lights of Los Angeles. On the plane ride, when those inevitable doubts crept in, I kept telling myself, "You won't be in England for long. Soon you'll be back in L.A." Yet somehow I knew that I was only kidding myself. Deep down I felt that I'd never come back—at least not as the same man. Something inside told me that England would be the beginning of a whole new chapter of my life. I knew it would be a journey into the future as well as the past.

Simon, my first British friend, was waiting for me when I landed in London. As we walked through Heathrow Airport, I gave up trying to plan this adventure. I had a feeling that it was already planned for me by a travel agent you couldn't find in any phone book.

◎

The minute I stepped outside the airport, I felt a bit giddy, because England was exactly like what I'd read about in my books. Everything was gray and damp on this mid-December day, which was a stark contrast to the bright and sunny weather I'd just left in California. However, I found the light drizzle to be refreshing on my tired face as we walked. Immediately, I felt myself drawn in by the mystery of this place.

Once we arrived in Bristol, I started to acclimate to my surroundings. During the day, I'd search out the used bookshops and browse through their dusty shelves looking for treasures. When I got thirsty or hungry, I'd go to one of the many coffeehouses and sit and read. It was such a novelty to wander into a real English pub and order a pint. All those books I'd read while living in California had come to life, and I felt as if I'd slipped into my own fantasy . . . except this was real, right down to the sticky floors in the pubs and the fish and chips served with salt and vinegar.

I felt like a little kid, because around every corner was something that caught my eye, whether it was an intricately carved stone fence or a fierce-looking gargoyle designed to spill out rainwater from the gutters perched high over the streets. I suddenly remembered how, as a child, I drew endless images that had no direct connection to my life. I began to wonder if any of them could be linked to the historical journey I was embarking on now. I made a mental note to find my old sketchbooks when I returned home and compare them with the many photographs I was now taking.

Before long, I started inquiring about Spiritualist churches, and it turned out that there were ten to choose from, right in Bristol! I wasted no time in making my way to one. It was a big moment for me, because this would be my first time in a real Spiritualist church. I expected to hesitate as I approached the entrance, but my feet didn't stop—they practically ran through those doors, with anticipation being their only guide.

Two women greeted me and immediately noticed my accent. I braced myself, fully preparing to be told that only members should enter. "Welcome, friend," they said. "You can sit where you like."

I noticed that everything from the pews to the brightly colored stained-glass windows looked like our churches back home. Awestruck that I was finally here, but not quite knowing what to expect, I took a seat.

The evening's services began with the church's president speaking for a moment, and then the medium was introduced. She was a short, well-dressed woman who looked like someone's "Mum." I found out that besides clairvoyance, it was also up to the medium to give an "inspired address," which meant that spirit would inspire her with images and words. Words just seemed to flow from this medium, and strangely, it seemed like she was talking directly to me. It was as if she knew what I needed to hear *at that exact moment.*

Eventually, she started her demonstration, which included connecting some of the members of the congregation with their loved ones who had passed. I imagined that if a Spiritualist received a message, they'd go home and tell their families, "I heard from Dad this evening," and another family member would respond, "Oh, yes? How is he, and what did he say?"

Spiritualists are raised to believe in the continuity of life, and mediums aren't celebrities to them—they're just messengers.

I was hooked, attending church regularly over the following months. Several times the mediums picked me out of the crowd, delivering a message from my grandfather or another relative. One even told me, "Young man, you have beautiful colors around you. Someday *you* will be up here doing this work."

There it was again—encouragement to move ahead. But no words were more important than those of a well-known medium visiting the church one evening—a man who would never know how influential he would be in my life.

The evening began with this man's wonderful way of working with the congregation and commanding the platform. Then he pointed straight at me. "You, sir! Yes, *you!* You were born with the gift of Spirit."

All heads in the church turned to face me, which is when I finally realized that he was talking about me. He added, "I also have your guide here with me, and after the service, I'll speak to you about him."

As soon as the service ended, I introduced myself, and he said, "I don't usually do this, but your guide is very strong and really wants me to tell you about him."

I could only nod because I was spellbound.

"Your guide is a Tibetan monk," he continued. "He's working with you and says that you are exactly where you should be at this point in your development. His message is simple: 'All you need to do is let go and trust.'"

This was my first introduction to one of my guides. (Later, I'd find that I have three of them.) Of course, I'd read a lot about spirit guides, but this was just the evidence I'd hoped to hear. I remembered that when I was a child, I often dreamed of praying men with shaved heads and colorful robes. Now, of course, I realize that they were Tibetan monks . . . and one of them was my guide.

I vowed to listen to my guide and do exactly as I was told: *Let go and trust.* Of course, that's always easier said than done.

— ◎ —

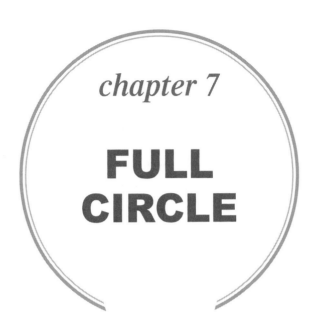

chapter 7

FULL
CIRCLE

I KNEW THAT I NEEDED TO SIT
for a longer reading with an experienced medium. I mentioned
to a lovely woman named Margaret, who was then the
regional secretary for the Spiritualist National Union (SNU),
how much I wanted to study mediumship in the UK. She suggested that I meet Joan Lambert, who had a great reputation
and a huge following.

My mind was racing throughout the drive across South
Wales because I knew that this was an important next step.
This was my first serious reading with a medium, and the student within me wanted to observe her style and dissect how
she received messages and passed the information on to me.

Joan greeted me at the door, and I found her to be an
immaculate, polite, and petite woman, with a warm smile and
a strong Welsh accent. Her home was very inviting, and it
included a reading room that was warm and peaceful, filling

me with a tranquility I'd never experienced before. Joan informed me that the actual reading would take place in her private consulting room upstairs. What she *didn't* tell me right away was how Spirit would make its presence known. For example, the lights in her home kept flickering (which I thought was awesome).

In a soft voice, Joan mentioned that my relatives were coming through to her. First, she brought through my mother's father, picking up his nationality and confirming that he'd died instantly from an aneurysm more than 50 years ago. Joan spoke about how particular he was about keeping his shoes shiny, even though he was a man who worked with his hands and the earth. Since he'd died before I was born, it was difficult for me to confirm some of her findings, but I knew that when I got home, I'd immediately delve into some family history to check out what she'd said. (Sometimes research is necessary to discover what's true.) However, Joan did give me some definite facts that I could confirm at once. "You were named after him, correct?" she asked, not really needing me to respond because she already knew the answer.

"Correct," I finally whispered.

Without giving me any notice that she was switching gears, she began to talk about my own psychic abilities. "I'm seeing wonderful colored lights around you, which means that you're psychically aware." She went on to describe where I was going in my life and the options for my future.

Next, she connected with a close friend who had died some years earlier. "I have a friend of yours here, and I believe he passed as a young man. I'm seeing the letter *J,* but his name isn't John. He says that you'd know him by his music and his communication background. I believe he's showing me a radio. He also wants to thank you for the flower you gave his mother at his funeral."

I think I picked up my jaw off the ground. All of this was true.

My friend Jamie did pass as a young man, and he was known for his musical background; he also used his wonderful deep voice in his job as an announcer for radio stations. Yes, I did bring one flower to his funeral in order to give it to his mother—a perfect white rose.

Even though I was already rather impressed with her, the most fascinating part of the sitting was when Joan brought through two of my guides. She explained that they were from Egypt and Tibet. Suddenly I understood why I'd always felt such an affinity with these places, even though I'd never been there. Joan reinforced what I already knew about my first guide, the Tibetan monk who was often by my side. Here he was again, making his presence known. Joan kept acknowledging the guides with little gestures and a few words here and there. "Yes, I'll tell him," she'd say, nodding to them before she'd turn back to me.

Joan continued to reveal more about my guides, who were clearly telling her about my tough childhood of poverty, loneliness, and my father's alcoholism. "You had to take care of your entire family," she said in the most sympathetic voice. She certainly hit a nerve, and I struggled to hold back the tears. No one could have possibly known the information that she relayed to me in the privacy of that room. Everything she was telling me rang true. I didn't even have to try to make it fit—it just did.

Joan reminded me that my guides were mine for life; and they'd always be there to support, guide, and protect me. They told her that there were many things they'd teach me in the future. She corrected herself. "No, wait a minute. They're telling me the *near* future."

I'm so glad that Joan was my first medium. I left her feeling as if I'd come home. She also helped me more than she could have ever known. She confirmed what I always knew—that we're all eternal and we do go on, and she inspired me and gave me the purpose to develop even more as a medium. I knew I wanted to give the same gift back to others.

I also left her home with a new sense of self-esteem. "It matters not where you've been, but where you are now," she said. "Use these words as your mantra—*I love and respect myself.*"

In addition, Joan encouraged me to get going on my own psychic path—and I was more eager now than ever. She immediately contacted Margaret, who said that she knew I had the ability, but I'd need some intense training. Joan picked it up from there and suggested that I sit in circle.

A development circle is when you sit in meditation with a group of other mediums and learn how to connect, reach out, and build a relationship with the spirit world. It's a great advantage to have an experienced medium running the circle, for they can assist with communication and cooperation with spirit guides and operators. They can also assist you in figuring out, usually in the beginning stages, what's spirit and what's coming from your own mind.

Learning the mechanics of mediumship was essential to me, as it should be to everyone who wants to develop their skills properly. I mentioned earlier that I wanted to be in control; to that end, I knew that sitting with like-minded people would help in the expansion of my abilities. Everyone sharing in each other's psychic energy was a thrilling idea to me.

When sitting in a circle, many people (including myself) experience various forms of psychic manifestations, including cold breezes, a slight draft around the feet and legs, sparkles of light, voices, or a cobweb sensation on the skin. The reason for this is that the spirit people use the group's combined psychic energy to draw close and strengthen their relationship with the sitters. I wasn't frightened at all by any of this because I'd be sitting with an experienced group who knew the basic rule: Development circles must be harmonious in *all* areas, and you must find the one that works for you. These include "open circles," which often take place in a church or a psychic-awareness class, and anyone can attend. There are also "home circles," which are by invitation only.

Margaret told me that she'd found a home circle that was willing to have me sit, but first I had to prove myself. She told me that this group had been sitting for five years, and they didn't let just anyone in.

I vividly remember the very first meeting I attended. It was in a typical English home, located in a part of Bristol called Brislington. After ushering me into a small waiting room on the side of the hall, Margaret briefly gave me an explanation about what would happen that evening, and more important, what was expected of me. She led me into the main room, and I was introduced to the seven other people who sat in a full circle. They were waiting for me.

Taking the only seat left, I tried to stop my knees from visibly shaking. The energy in the room was intense, charged, and full of love, due to the fact that the group had been meditating earlier to prepare to meet and work with me. That's one of the purposes of meditation—to fill the room with energy.

One by one, the group members introduced themselves, and then it was my turn to say hello. I gave them a brief summary of my life as a psychic and medium, and told the story of how I'd come to England. The words flowed from me, for I felt so open and free in this softly lit room with its sparse, yet comfortable, furnishings.

Next, the group leader explained what was about to happen. What followed was a bit like an audition without the lights or a stage. First, I was asked to do a short demonstration so the rest of the group could evaluate my skill level. The members wanted me to link with Spirit and pass the messages to everyone in the circle. Before I started, I was told that they'd send me their energy to elevate my senses.

We recited "The Lord's Prayer" in unison, and they gave me the nod to begin. It was strange for me to be on display in this way, and I could feel all eyes watching me closely. I fought to control my nerves and concentrated as hard as possible. Then I took a deep breath and closed my eyes.

At first, I felt nothing. Total silence.

I didn't hear the spirits—I just heard my own breathing, which sounded as if it was being played through an amplifier. I felt crushed with failure. But a middle-aged man named Peter helped me relax. He began to guide me, telling me to raise my consciousness higher. For a minute, I jokingly thought that "raising my consciousness" meant lifting my butt off the chair. What he really meant, of course, was to expand my thoughts to a higher realm and, at the same time, continue to expand my energy field.

I took another deep breath, and the room began to blur. I felt as though someone were standing behind me, but before I could say a word, the whole group spoke. "Hello, friend," they said.

At first, I didn't know whom they were greeting. *Did someone walk into the room? Should I open one eye?* Peter immediately interjected, "John, take your time and give us what you're receiving."

I relaxed, opened my mouth, and amazing words of inspiration just flowed from me. *Who was talking? Where were the words coming from?* This is what I meant early on about inspirational speaking. Slowly, I began to recite what was being given to me:

> *"Many people think strength is a rock or*
> *a tall tree, but the strength of the*
> *human heart is immeasurable.*
> *The sun bears down on you, with the*
> *light in which all things grow.*
> *Fear not when the cloud passes the sun,*
> *for you will know that the cloud will pass.*
> *We are coming through to you with*
> *a fluidity of a strong essence.*
> *Come forth and begin."*

Clearly, this group of seven had just projected me to a higher level of consciousness. All that psychic energy lifted my vibration to another level, and the best way I can describe it is to say that it's like having two personalities. It's not a split personality, but two separate ones. I was aware of what I was saying, but it was like I was standing back and somehow listening to myself. These weren't words I would normally use because I don't tend to speak in such a poetic fashion.

I could hear Margaret sitting in the corner, furiously sliding a pencil across a piece of paper so she could keep a record of what I was saying. Strangely, even though it seemed as if I were talking slower than usual, I wasn't afraid of what was happening to me. I can only liken the sensation to the feeling a child gets when his mother wraps her arms around him for comfort and protection. I felt that happy and secure.

Peter cut in again, saying, "What does it feel like to have Spirit speaking through you?"

I didn't quite know how to answer at first, but after a moment, I replied, "I can feel a Native American, tall and broad. I can also feel his culture all around me." This Native American was actually another one of my guides, and he'd just made himself known to me. (I later found out that it was his job to help me with inspirational speaking.)

"Break the connection now, John. It's time," Peter said. His voice took on a more forceful tone, so I didn't question his instructions.

Finally, the group thanked the spirit, and I found myself sitting there looking a little bewildered.

"What just happened?" I asked them.

"We'll discuss it all in circle shortly," Peter said.

I didn't have time to listen to the rest of his sentence because there was more. I closed my eyes again and quickly linked with an older woman who told me that she'd passed away in a nursing home. She was telling me that she didn't want to leave her house or her beloved garden. Then she said that she had a form of dementia. Her family thought that she'd lost her mind, so they made the decision to put her into the home.

Holding her off for a moment, I returned to myself because I wasn't sure if I should continue or not. I asked the circle if someone understood what I was saying: "Can anyone take this, please?"

One of the women spoke up and asked me to continue. Peter smiled at me as a signal to finish this one because he knew that I had another link.

As the old woman gave me more evidence, it was clear

that she wanted me to communicate that she was happy now and forgave her family. She also wanted them to let go of their guilt for putting her in the nursing home. She understood why they'd made such a difficult decision, but she wanted them to know that she was back in her garden in the spirit world. She was no longer suffering any pain, and she wanted to send her love to a certain woman in the circle. The love that I was feeling could only be from a mother.

With her message communicated to her loved one, her mission was accomplished. One breath later, she was gone, and I was alone again. I wondered how I'd done. *Did I pass the test?*

There were no immediate answers because I was asked to leave the room. The circle was going to discuss me. I got up, thanked them, and slipped out into the small waiting area. It seemed as if I waited for hours, and then there was Margaret, asking me to come back in. Of course, I was expecting to be let down gently and told to come back in a few years when I'd improved. That's not what happened.

"Welcome to our circle, John," they said.

I was honored and privileged.

Margaret then showed me the notes she'd taken. To this day, I have those pages that mean so much to me because they're part of my own history. I must say that my first night in the circle left me quite excited, and assisted in my confidence. I was also informed that some people had to sit in circle for *years* before they even started their work as a medium.

The group wanted to know if I was committed to sitting each and every week at the same time. What we'd be doing is setting up an appointment with Spirit, so I was told that if I was late, I'd find the door locked.

Late? Forget it. Who was I to leave the spirit world waiting?

◉

Being accepted into a circle meant that I'd have to extend my stay in England. Once again, I was in luck, because a friend of mine from Boston needed a place to stay in California while she decided to make the move or not. So we decided that she'd rent my apartment. Eureka! I was sure of one thing: Something else was at work here. Again, I believe there are no accidents.

Those few scheduled weeks in England had turned into months and several odd jobs, which meant that I made enough money for my rent and food. People were incredibly generous and were always offering me meals and rides. I sat in a circle every week and heeded the warning that I was given on that first day. I was never late.

The results were beyond my expectations, as my abilities and techniques were noticeably improving over time. The leader of the circle had advised me not to emulate anyone else, for I needed to expand my abilities in my own way. I should just learn to open myself to Spirit. And so, with each session in the circle, I'd raise my consciousness to a higher level and learn to blend with those on the Other Side.

I'd feel the spirit people draw close. My body's vibrations would speed up as the images slowly formed in my mind's eye. It was so important in those early days to spend as much time as possible with experienced mediums to make sure that I didn't pick up any bad habits. I also had to learn the right protocol and code of conduct of doing such work. But after the circle, we'd drink tea (how British) and talk about the various messages we'd received that evening.

Meanwhile, Margaret and I had become good friends, and she told me that she'd been appointed president of her own

Spiritualist church in a small town called Devizes. Over the following months, she introduced me to many different mediums who served at her church, including Gordon Smith, a charismatic man from Glasgow who would even do his demonstrations in a full traditional Scottish kilt. That was a first!

Gordon and I stayed in contact, and he said that I could come to Scotland anytime. He also suggested something I was beginning to hear many times to the point where I couldn't ignore it: "John, you should really go and study at the Arthur Findlay College."

I kept hearing about this school, which was dedicated to teaching classes on communicating with Spirit and refining one's psychic abilities. This wasn't a place for learning English or mathematics. It was for learning about life and death.

"You mean that they have a school for people like me? One that teaches the exact subjects I'm interested in? Sign me up!" I said.

A few weeks after I filled out the application, I received a slim envelope in the mail. Inside was a note that said: "Welcome to Arthur Findlay College."

chapter 8

SPIRIT BOOT CAMP

"ALL ABOARD!" YELLED THE CONDUCTOR as I embarked upon my train ride to the Arthur Findlay College at Stansted Hall. As usual, my head was full of questions and doubts: I wondered if I'd be good enough for this place and if I'd be able to keep up with my fellow students. I breathed deeply and tried to clear my mind of all its clutter.

Hours later, my fears had all but vanished as I stood outside Stansted Hall. A beautifully aged stone mansion built in 1871, the building was situated on 15 acres of private land with its own chapel, and the sweeping grounds were a breathtaking mixture of colorful shrubs and grasses that seemed to glow. It was almost as if the trees wanted to keep this place a secret from the rest of the world.

I tried to prevent my heart from doing cartwheels in my chest as I stared up at the heavy doors of the mansion. When I stepped inside, I noticed that the wood and marble floors seemed to stretch on forever and led in all directions, and the towering ceilings were framed and accented with beautiful hand-carved artwork.

Let me make one thing perfectly clear: There was nothing spooky about this place. There were no spiders or cobwebs in the corners, no white sheets covering the furniture, and certainly no smoke rising from the floor. In fact, the front room was brightly lit by the sun beaming through the tall windows. The library was fit for a king, with its stunning brick fireplace, and the book-lined shelves caught my attention. I noted that among the many ancient volumes were some shiny new covers, which meant that the school was progressive. I felt as if the place was a storehouse of knowledge.

Through one of the windows, I spotted the beautiful chapel where students participated in Sunday services and demonstrations of mediumship. I'd already read in the brochure they'd sent me that the chapel was open to the public, who came from miles around to hear mediums and other speakers deliver messages from loved ones. The school even had its own pub, an area dedicated to winding down at the end of a long day.

The college was originally a mansion for Arthur Findlay, a man who devoted a major part of his life to the studies of life after death. When he passed on in 1964, he bequeathed Stansted Hall (as it was then known) to the Spiritualist National Union. The school is now named after him (although everyone just fondly calls it "Stansted"), which I'm sure would please Findlay, because he always wanted his home to become a training facility for mediums and be dedicated to the advancement of the psychic sciences.

The facilities are unequaled anywhere in the world. The mechanics of mediumship, spiritual healing, and psychic awareness and its unfoldment are the top courses, and the training is the best I've ever come across. Renowned mediums of the highest caliber travel hundreds of miles to teach there, and some of the very best in the world have also attended the school. I considered myself fortunate to be following in these prestigious footsteps.

I felt my blood course thrrough my body as I walked through the halls. I was told about a famous photograph that featured a spirit and their infamous "tulip tree." Hundreds of beautiful pink and lilac flowers decorated the tree like fragrant ornaments that didn't grow anywhere else on Earth—and one could see the very visible outline of a man dressed in 18th-century period clothes standing in front of the tree.

Eighty new students were to be enrolled in Stansted on this day, so we all hurried downstairs for the mandatory orientation in the grand hall. It was a veritable League of Nations, for students from all over the world were attending. I heard French, German, English, Swiss, Spanish, Japanese, and Australian accents, along with the different dialects of the many British who were there. I was one of two Americans, yet as soon as I opened my mouth, the students quickly dubbed me "the Yank."

The program leader called the orientation to order, and we were introduced to all the teachers. All were women, dressed impeccably in crisp skirts and ironed blouses. Some even had scarves adorning their necks, and I couldn't help but notice how neat they were, right down to their perfectly shined shoes. In fact, the whole scene was perfect.

"Ladies and gentlemen, welcome to Stanstcd," our program director announced before quickly running through the school's rules.

We were instructed to always come to classes and meals right on time. No late-night parties, no smoking, no walking the halls in the wee hours of the night, and most definitely, no leaving the grounds without permission. All 80 of us were now the responsibility of the school, 24 hours a day.

Next, we had to fill out a lengthy questionnaire about our experiences and knowledge of psychic ability and mediumship. Once the teachers reviewed our forms, we'd be assigned our tutors based on the level of our experiences.

My time would be spent with Jean, a medium with a great reputation, who was also an excellent speaker and minister. She'd been a member of the Spiritualist movement for many years and had a beautiful air of authority about her that was evident with every move she made and each word she spoke. Standing erect with perfect posture and precise pitch, she appeared to be a soldier for Spirit.

The next order of business was sorting out my classes. My curriculum consisted of meditation exercises, philosophy, psychic and mediumistic development, colors, symbology, public speaking, demonstration skills, guides and helpers, and circle work. Also included were classes in clairvoyance, clairaudience, and clairsentience. I also signed up for my soon-to-be favorite class: "Linking with Spirit."

Every student was required to attend mandatory lectures that focused on the huge responsibility of doing this work. The college also focused on the code of conduct all mediums should uphold. I didn't consider any of this to be a waste of time. In fact, I was so excited to get up each morning that I practically ran to my classes.

A typical classroom experience was like nothing else in the world. Stansted really promoted knowledge and sharing—they didn't just believe in an instructor standing in front of a class, but wanted students to learn from their very eclectic peers. To that end, we formed groups, quickly telling each other a little about ourselves.

I was placed in a beginner's group, which suited me just fine. I wanted to take it slow, and I needed structure—I knew that some of the answers I'd been seeking my entire life would be found within these walls. Little did I know that the school would treat us beginners as if we were practicing mediums. The idea was to push us further than we ever thought was possible and to use all the time available, from 9 A.M. to 8 P.M. each and every day, while we were there.

With its strict schedule and many classes, I fondly referred to Stansted as "Spirit Boot Camp." It was daunting and exhausting, but in the best possible way. And just like a sponge, I rapidly soaked up all of the incredible knowledge available to me (I'll share some specific techniques I learned in Part III). But it wasn't all work and no play. At night we'd gravitate to the pub for a little mixing and mingling.

On one of my first nights at Stansted, I found myself lying in bed, looking out the window at the brightly lit moon. I suddenly felt as if I was farther away from home than I'd ever been in my entire life. I was quite homesick, but the moment of sadness was cut abruptly short. I started to hear whispering in my ear, which sounded like voices welcoming me.

As time passed, the tasks became tougher at Spirit Boot Camp. Before I knew it, we were having practice demonstrations where each of us beginners took turns being the mediums or the speakers.

My first time up in front of all my fellow students was a moment I'll never forget. I was a bundle of nerves as I walked to the podium, but it turned out that I'd have to wait my turn. I was told to take my seat, which was on the platform toward the back. I guess I got a little too close to the edge of the stage because I fell off it backwards, legs flying in the air and chair landing on top of me. Talk about embarrassing! My crimson face could only peek up over the back of the platform to see that everyone was laughing so hard that tears were running down their faces. At which point, I only had one choice. I began to laugh hysterically, too, while rubbing my aching head. I sure raised the energy in *that* room!

One of the highlights of my time at Stansted was being assigned to a course in demonstration taught by Joan Lambert, who had given me my first reading. I was thrilled that she was teaching at the college. One night Joan invited the entire school to attend one of her sessions. She began the proceedings by asking a student named Cheryl to come to the front and join her onstage. Poor Cheryl was very nervous because we weren't in a small classroom—the great hall was filled to capacity with students, tutors, and friends who were now looking at her and waiting to see if she could link with spirit and pass along any messages.

Cheryl began by offering some evidence of a spirit, but her words were slow and scattered. She was becoming more nervous by the moment, and when this happens, the flow of information can get clogged. Joan immediately stood up, placed herself directly behind Cheryl, and placed her hand on Cheryl's back. She spoke slowly and told Cheryl to relax and breathe correctly. Joan's actions sent energy to Cheryl and guided her back into the link.

We watched in fascination as all of Cheryl's blocks slowly started to disappear and she began to see more vividly. Joan seemed to be focusing on something as well. Suddenly, they were speaking together in perfect unison. They were totally in sync with one another. Both women were describing a spirit and a room in a house—the details of the room and the furniture formed a perfect image.

I'd seen this awesome sight of two mediums receiving the same information before, called a "double link." Both Cheryl and Joan were tapping in to the same spirit, or as I like to put it, they were both on the same phone line. It truly was something special to watch.

Joan continued to guide Cheryl, asking her to look around and describe what she was seeing. As time passed, Cheryl's face became luminous, and she started to cry. She was taught to see with new eyes, and her tears were those of pure joy. She went on with the rest of the message alone and delivered it to the right person in the audience.

When she was finished, the applause was thunderous. Of course, the Boston boy in me also let out a huge whistle. So much for being "the shy Yank."

As my time at Stansted drew to a close, I needed to pull together everything I'd been taught in order to give a demonstration in front of the entire school. It was like a final exam, except there was no research paper or multiple-choice questions. This was a practical test, which I called "the real thing."

That morning, the bright, sunny hall was filled with eager faces—some highly advanced in their abilities, while others were just beginners. I felt like a fourth grader about to give his first speech, and I worried about freezing up in front of my fellow students. I'd never given a demonstration in front of such a large group. Could I get a link and deliver a proper message? And what if I fell off the stage again? Thankfully, Jean, my tutor, was there to support me as I sweated it out, waiting for my name to be called.

"Ladies and gentleman, John Holland from America will demonstrate next," said the presenter.

All I could do was stand up, take a step forward, and suck in a deep breath. Immediately I started my clairvoyance, but I felt as though I were under a microscope. I knew the one golden rule: When you study mediumship at Stansted, the focus is on accurate information and delivering as much of it as possible. The tutors wouldn't settle for anything less. You couldn't get away with being vague and saying, "Oh, your grandma is here and she loves you." The tutors would frown and say, "That's not how it's done. Evidence! Evidence! That's what we must strive for and always give."

I don't know why I had any doubts—I felt myself linking almost right away. Images and feelings were coming quickly, and I knew my job was to sort them out. I tried to remember everything I'd been taught, but the information was eluding me. My nerves were blocking the link, but luckily I was able to control my emotions. The jumpiness was actually pushed away by a warm feeling that quickly came over me: Spirit was drawing closer and would help me deliver the message.

After what seemed like an eternity, I became aware of a gentleman coming close to me, and I knew that he was someone's grandfather. I could feel his kindness all around me, along with how frail he'd been just before he passed. Some spirits impress you with memories of their physical body as a way to identify them, so I knew that this was an elderly man who had trouble walking later in his life. He showed me his favorite brown leather chair and footrest, mentioning that this was his favorite place in the house. He told me that he loved his small brick fireplace, adored his family, and that his name was Roger.

"Roger worked in a shipyard," I told the audience. "He lived a full life into his 80s." Yes, now I could feel his age overshadowing my own body. I wasn't *becoming* Roger, but I did feel weak and tired. It was as though my legs had suddenly lost all their strength. That's how close he was to me.

I stared into the audience and waited for someone to raise a hand to acknowledge that they could understand the name Roger. No one moved, but I couldn't let doubts overcome me. So I took a deep breath and started again . . . then I just knew. I pointed to the back of the room and asked, "Did you have a grandfather who didn't allow you to sit in his chair?"

A young student who had been daydreaming looked up when all eyes turned to stare at him. Once again, I gave the information, and a look of acknowledgment and surprise came over his face. "That's my Grandpa Roger!" he exclaimed. "No one could sit in Gramps's chair or use his footrest. That was his property only. And he did work in a shipyard when he was younger."

Roger wanted to come to his favorite grandson and encourage him to continue his education. "Your grandfather says that you shouldn't drop out of school at this time," I told the young man. "The financial assistance you're seeking will come through. He also wants you to send his love to your mother."

It turns out that this fellow and his Gramps had enjoyed a great bond when Roger was alive. "I still think of Gramps all the time," the young man said as a smile played on his lips. "We'd talk for hours—and I still talk to him whenever I feel confused or I need a little help."

The messages from Roger soon faded once his grandson assured him that he'd stay in school. Then I felt the energy pull back and become weaker until it was gone. I glanced up at the large clock on the wall. It seemed as if only seconds had passed since I'd stepped up to the podium, but actually I'd been speaking for quite a long time.

During the time I linked with Roger, I noticed that my speech had become much faster and my own energy was quickening. As soon as the spirit communicator stepped back, I slowed down. It was like something inside was down-shifting.

My final exam was over, yet I wasn't sure how I'd done. I couldn't even look at my tutors, but fortunately I didn't have to wait long before one of them leaned toward me. She placed a hand on my shoulder and proudly exclaimed, "You did very well, Mr. Holland! Very well, indeed."

That was the signal that my time at Stansted had come to an end. The best lesson I learned there is that each of us is born with our own special gift, and to find it, we must first find our own spirit within. The need to awaken our spiritual awareness is vital, and our progression here on Earth depends on it.

The tutors advised us to take it slow after leaving the college, since after studying and using our psychic senses so much, we were now "extra sensitive." They also said, "The outside world may be too much at first, and you might need to slowly integrate back into your own personal life. Just remember all that you've learned, and continue on your path."

I made many friends at the college, and I'll always treasure the experiences and knowledge that was put before me. I still look at my journals from time to time in order to be transported back to a place that I'll hold close to my heart forever.

Thank you, Stansted.

— ◎ —

chapter 9

BOSTON CALLS

AS I SAT IN THE LOUNGE AT Heathrow Airport, I heard an announcement that snapped me out of my reverie: "Flight 721, now boarding for Los Angeles." What was supposed to have been just six weeks in England had turned into almost two fascinating years. But in my heart, I knew that it was time to head home. I wasn't the same man anymore, and I had to get my priorities in order. So my first stop would be L.A., and then I'd be on my way back to Boston. My mom was suffering from a lung condition, and I knew that I needed to be closer to my family again.

As I sat on the plane, I let my mind wander back to my last few days in England. I'd visited a church in Bristol that I hadn't been to yet (believe it or not), and as always, I was invited to sit, meditate, and join them in their circle. At first, I sat quietly and listened to the other members give the evidence that they were receiving. Some said they were seeing beautiful colors, while others were talking about rainbows, birds, and forests. I wondered if I should share that I was receiving much more than colors.

The spirit of an elderly man had started to link with me, and I knew that he was related to someone in the room. The link was very strong: I could clearly see him dressed in immaculate white vestments, with a purple stole with two yellow crucifixes on each end draped around his shoulders. I knew he was associated with the church.

He came across with a scowl on his face, but I knew that somehow these frown lines resulted from age rather than from his disposition or personality. He eventually smiled, and I felt his face light up as though there was a glowing light about him. This made him appear to have a peaceful serenity that was being released from his very being.

He wanted me to pass on this message to someone in the circle: "Just tell her that it's better to have loved and lost than to have never loved at all." I'd heard this saying many times, of course, and I asked myself if this was coming *to* or *from* me . . . but I knew it wasn't from me.

He continued by saying, "Tell her how thankful I am for her taking care of everything, and I will always be with her. Thank her for the angel."

I decided to tell the members in the circle what I was receiving, and as always, I asked, "Does anyone understand this?"

I noticed one woman at the far end start to wipe her eyes, and she confirmed that it was her dad whom I was linking with. "He was a bishop in the Church of England, and he was buried in his complete ceremonial vestment robes, including his favorite purple stole," she said. When her father was ill, she took care of him, and when he passed a few years earlier, she made all the funeral arrangements exactly as he'd requested. When she'd stood over his casket saying good-bye, she'd taken her favorite pin, affixed it to his stole, and said, "Now you can be with your angels, Daddy. I love you." The pin was of an angel.

Just hearing that he appreciated her honoring his last wishes brought this woman much joy. She thanked me and said that this was the most beautiful message—the one she'd been waiting for since his passing. It was a heartwarming experience.

Next, I'd taken a short trip to Scotland to visit medium Gordon Smith on a whim. Little did I know that he'd introduce me to the congregation and then call me up to the platform to give a message. He certainly caught me by surprise, and at first, I tried to back out of it.

He didn't want to hear it. "John, you can do this. Come on now!"

I stood there and looked out at the audience. Would they understand me? Yes, my nerves were kicking in again. Mercifully, I was drawn to an elderly woman in the congregation as I started to link with her mom. I felt as though the mother must have been gone a while, since the lady in front of me was easily in her 80s.

I gathered myself together and said, "I have your mom here, and she's telling me that she's with your dad and her family. She's also talking about the horses and how she taught you to ride."

The woman nodded and said, "Please continue, son."

I wasn't sure of the next message. "Can this be right? Your mom is telling me that she *just* crossed over, less than six months ago."

"That's right, young man," she said with a slight giggle. "My mom passed at the age of 102!"

The entire audience burst into spontaneous applause, but I wasn't interrupted, so I went on. "Your mom wants you to know that she has her youth back. She's fine, and she's with all her loved ones who passed so many years before her," I told the beaming daughter.

As I thought about these people, I realized how much I longed to be with my *own* loved ones.

I arrived back in Los Angeles, but before I knew it, I was packing my bags again. I said good-bye to my friends and favorite spots, including the windswept beach in Santa Monica. I was nervous going back to Boston, which I'd left 12 years earlier. *Will I reconnect with my family and all the memories that I've left behind?* I wondered. *Will I be accepted back as a medium?* The people of California had lived up to their reputation for being free, open-minded, and into the whole New Age mentality, but I wasn't so sure about the conservative city of Boston.

However, I knew that I now had experience, and my guides would help me spread the word of Spirit to a city that I hoped was ready to at least explore the concept of life after death. I made it my goal to take it one day at a time.

I have to be honest and say that it wasn't an easy adjustment to come back to Boston, which is a relatively small but fast-paced city. I got an apartment in Cambridge about five miles from my mom. I wanted to be close in case she needed me, which was the main reason for this homecoming. I also found a regular nine-to-five office job, and I slowly started to build a reputation in Boston as a psychic and medium. So once again, I found myself working two jobs.

Exposure came my way when the local newspapers did a couple of stories on me and a few radio stations had me on to do readings live on the air. Being on the radio was a brand-new experience, and it helped me receive and give out information quickly—there was no time to talk to the audience, as this was live radio.

I was lucky enough to have found a job where they knew what I did on the side and weren't put off by it. It didn't hurt that my bosses and fellow employees saw me in the newspaper and were fascinated to be working next to someone who was getting media attention. But I didn't take the "medium" into work with me—from nine to five, I was just John.

A turning point in my life occurred on an ordinary evening at rush hour. Everyone at the subway station was pushing and shoving, and it had been a particularly busy day at my day job. I knew I had to find my second wind because as soon as I got home, I had to go to work again doing readings.

That night, the train was packed and I was lucky to get a seat. As we lurched out of the station, I glanced to my left and noticed that the seat next to me remained empty. I shrugged and went back to the book I was reading. I looked up to see an elderly nun in her full habit standing in front of me.

"Hello, young man," she said. "You have a nice face. Is the seat next to you taken?"

"No, Sister, please go right ahead," I said, sliding over a few more inches to make more room for her.

As the train moved along, I could feel the nun looking at me while I was trying to read. I turned to her and noticed a pair of the bluest, kindest eyes I'd ever seen—in fact, she seemed to be looking right inside of me. "My name is Sister Agnes, but most people call me Aggie for short," she said.

"Hi, I'm John," I replied. Apparently she was going to talk the whole way home, so I prepared myself to politely listen.

"Can you guess what I do for a living?" she asked.

"Well, let me see . . . um . . . you're a schoolteacher?" I said with a smile.

Sister Aggie returned the grin and informed me, "No, I help people who are ill and living in hospices or in the hospital. I help them get ready to die and cross over. Many people call me a 'Counselor for God.'"

My mouth dropped open, and all I could say in my best Boston accent was an excited, "Sistah! Did you evah sit in the right seat! You get them before they go, and I get them after! I'm a medium."

Since she was such a special person who did a particularly difficult type of work, I asked her how she got through the tough times.

"My job is to give others love and compassion. I'm sure you can relate, John, as the work you're doing is important, and I know you're good at it," she said, looking gently into my eyes.

How does she know how good I am? I wondered. *She has no idea who I am!*

"You're giving people 'Memory Days,'" she continued.

"What do mean by that, Sister?" I asked.

"John, some days come and some days go," she quickly replied. "People don't realize that every day is a new beginning and a chance to start over. There are days that people remember forever, while other days simply slip away into their yesterdays and tomorrows. You never know when you're giving someone a 'Memory Day.' It can be an act of kindness, a trip to the country, or something as simple as helping an elderly woman with her groceries. People remember certain days for the rest of their lives."

She paused to let her words sink in. "We take these memories with us when we pass," she said, "and I do believe that we review our lives with all our faults and accomplishments. Why not have the best memories by our side, and try to give good ones to whomever we can?"

As she spoke, I knew that we were both on the same spiritual wavelength.

"All we can do is our best. That's why you and I are here—to do the best possible job with the time we're given," she concluded as I realized that we'd pulled into Harvard Square Station.

I wished her the very best and said a heartfelt good-bye. Sister Aggie stood up and tossed me her biggest smile. "Bless you, John. Keep up the faith," she said.

"You too, Sister," I replied, looking down for only a split second. When I looked up, she was gone. Sure, it was crowded in the station, but I didn't even see her blend into the crowd. I knew that I couldn't explain her presence, but I'd never forget her because she'd left me with my own "Memory Day."

Now I know that our meeting was meant to be, for I obviously needed to hear what Sister Aggie had to say at that precise time in my life. I knew that I wouldn't be working two jobs for much longer because I had to follow my true calling.

One evening while I was having dinner, the phone rang. The voice on the other end said, "Hello, John? This is Anne from the television show *Unsolved Mysteries*."

I think I almost dropped the phone. "Yes, may I help you?" I tried to say calmly.

"Someone sent in a letter about you and your accident and how that has affected your abilities," she said. "We're very interested in putting your story on our show."

It's funny, but people who haven't seen my story on *Unsolved Mysteries* have asked what mystery I solved. Well, *I* was the mystery! My segment explained how my car accident turned up my abilities to help people connect with those who have passed. I guess that was enough of a mystery for the producers.

But before any of that could happen, I had to get my story on TV in the first place. I never realized how complicated this would be. I had to give the producers a list of clients to be interviewed, but even that wasn't enough confirmation.

"John, we understand that these clients say you have these abilities, but we'll need to test you ourselves," said one of the production assistants.

I totally understood their position, and I wanted to help out in any way I could. I had the utmost respect for the show and its credibility, as it has helped to educate so many people, even reuniting families by giving nationwide attention to the plight of missing children.

One of the producers asked me if I'd be willing to read for their assistant. I agreed because I wanted to be involved in the whole concept of the story and the way I'd be portrayed. I did request that they not make the story too eerie or ghostly because that's not what I wanted the public to think about mediumship, and it certainly wasn't me.

Due to time constraints, I ended up doing the reading over the phone. I started to tell this young production assistant about her life and her family, explaining how she got to this point and how she began working in the entertainment business. I gave her personal and very identifying facts about the people around her, but when I gave her the last name of one of her colleagues—something I couldn't have possibly known because I knew nothing about this woman—that sealed the deal.

About 15 minutes into the reading, the assistant asked me to stop because she was getting a little nervous, which was understandable given that she'd never had a reading or even dealt with a psychic before. She couldn't figure out how I could possibly have known private things about her that no one else knew. Before she hung up, she said that she'd report back to the producers and they'd be in touch.

A few days later, I received a call saying that they'd like me to do the show. Naturally, I was elated.

They filmed the actual piece in California and cast a professional actor to play me (what a trip!). One scene depicted me in the hotel giving readings, and another re-enacted the car accident. My friend Joyce played herself and gave tips to the actor who was playing me on how I worked while giving readings. They even called Adrian, who played herself in the scene where she found her dad's poem hidden in the book.

After all that filming, we had to wait several months for the show to air. When it did, my family and I sat glued to the tube. I was very pleased with the results because they did a fantastic job and never portrayed my world in a weird way. Of course, I wasn't at all prepared for what came next.

After the show aired, I was flooded with phone calls, letters, and e-mails from all over the country. Some people asked me to find their lost children; some wanted my blessing, as if I had some divine power; and some were treasure hunters, asking me to help them find lost riches. I knew the show attracted a big audience, but this was crazy. It was too much attention, too soon. I tried to do what I could, but I was soon becoming mentally and physically exhausted because there just weren't enough hours in the day.

To help me cope, I reached out to Suzane Northrop, a very well-known trance medium in New York who had been doing this work for 25 years. I'd seen her in Boston, and I was amazed by the evidence she gave in her tell-it-like-she-saw-it way. I ended up sending her publicist a videotape and letter to pass on to Suzane.

A short time later, I received a call from Suzane herself, and we agreed to have lunch in New York City. When we met, I noted that (like me) she was just a normal, down-to-earth person. I immediately felt comfortable with her and knew that we'd be able to talk. As it turned out, we spoke for hours, although she didn't get to do much talking—she just listened as I poured out my story.

When I was finished, she asked, "What do *you* want, John? Where do you want this to go? You can take control."

Part of taking control was realizing that since my mother's health had improved, I was free to leave Boston. So I moved to the nearby state of New Hampshire (to get out of the city and be closer to nature), where I set up my new office as a medium and sorted through a huge pile of requests for my services.

I knew that my life as a medium had truly just begun.

— ◎ —

part II

spirit
CONNECTIONS

chapter 10

I HEAR A VOICE

WHEN I'M LINKING WITH THE Other Side, information is delivered to me in a number of ways—through words, feelings, images, smells, and even tastes. Sometimes I don't even know sometimes what these sensory messages mean because they're only meant for the spirit's loved one to understand. It's almost as if I'm a radio and the information is coming through some special spiritual airwave that I psychically hear, for the sole purpose of passing it on to the person who needs to hear it the most.

Each sitting is like its own program, and it can be filled with both laughter and tears. Some people make an appointment with me to "tune in" for a sense of closure or as a way for their loved one to show them that they are, and always will be, connected to each other.

I hope that sharing some of my most amazing client stories will help you to know that you're never truly alone. What

follows are the accounts that have especially touched my
heart, and in reading them, I hope that you'll also pause to consider the wonder all around you . . . even if you can't see it—
at least not right away.

Healing Waters

There's something peaceful and healing about watching
the sun dance on crystal-blue water. I've had a love affair with
the ocean for most of my life, and I currently live near water,
enjoying its energy and the calming effect that it has upon me.

I got my chance to really experience the splendor of the
ocean when Suzane Northrop called to ask if I'd like to join
her as one of the featured mediums on a psychic healing cruise
to the Caribbean. I guess she was trusting her own intuition
that I could be of service to the guests and use my abilities
to assist with the healing that so many of them would need.

This wasn't a vacation for people who just liked lavish
buffets and dancing until dawn. It was to be a voyage for people who were hoping to link with someone who had passed.
Hopefully, the guests would return home with a souvenir they
couldn't buy in any store: knowledge and a possible connection with the Other Side.

The cruise was also for those who were interested in
developing their own intuitive abilities. So, apart from Suzane
and myself, there were also lecturers, mediums, healers,
motivational and empowerment experts, a bereavement counselor, psychics, and teachers who arrived from all parts of the
United States. All of us came together in the hopes of edu-
cating and empowering the attendees through intimate workshops and lectures.

As soon as we heard "Bon voyage," I was put to work, as the very first program called for Suzane and me to do a mediumship demonstration for the guests. There were 80 participants in all, so she and I were to take 40 guests each into separate rooms. Who went where was decided when the group was told to reach into a hat and pick one of two colors: The green group would go with Suzanne, and the red group would go with me. At the last minute, the cruise director did a little switch-a-roo—everyone who picked my color would now go with Suzane and vice versa—probably to ensure that the guests didn't switch colors to be with the medium they wanted. Of course, I knew that it didn't matter which group people were in—if they were supposed to get a message, they'd get it. But that last-minute switching proved to be very interesting indeed.

My group broke off and went into our own area, where I found myself gazing at 40 people whose faces were like hopeful question marks. It's funny how in these group settings you can almost feel the desire rumbling through the audience as each member hopes that the medium will connect with him or her. Unfortunately, it's not up to the medium—it's the choice of the spirit world when it will make itself known and who will be the "guest stars."

That night, so many people were counting on me to come up with the goods. I looked at my group swaying back and forth with the rocking of the boat and said to myself, "Please, God, help me get through this."

This was my first time on a cruise ship, so I tried to control my seasick stomach. I breathed deeply, reassuring myself that Spirit didn't mind traveling to the middle of the ocean. Almost as if to prove my point, I began to link almost immediately. I quietly whispered to myself, "Yes, I understand."

I met some fascinating people on the cruise, including Ron and Gail (more about them in the next chapter), who had traveled from Florida to attend the cruise with their best friends Sheryl and Mike—and let's just say that the four of them weren't aware of my work. In fact, they'd been hoping to land in Suzane's group, and had even switched color tags with some other people in order to ensure that they'd meet with her. At the last moment, when the cruise director did the flip-flop of groups, they were a bit disappointed.

As Gail admits today, "I didn't know this guy John or his capabilities, so I'm embarrassed to say that we finagled it to be with Suzane—but I guess we truly were supposed to be with John. It was almost as if that was decided before we even got on the cruise, because what happened that night changed all of our lives."

All four stopped whispering to each other when I looked in their direction and said, "A male is coming through to me calling out the name Scott. Does anyone here know someone by that name?"

Mike felt a little jolt. He had a son named Scott, but inside he felt anxious and didn't speak up. "I thought that Scott was such a common name—what were the chances he was talking about me?" he explained later.

"Now I'm hearing the name Patricia," I continued.

At that point, Mike and Sheryl's heads popped up. Mike's sister was named Patricia.

"I also have a mother and father figure who have crossed, and they're with their son who passed young," I said. "Who has the *M* name?"

Mike finally raised his hand. "I'm Mike. My son is named Scott. My sister is Patricia. My brother has passed, and so have my parents."

As Mike spoke, I kept tapping on my chest, knowing it was a heart attack that brought his brother to the Other Side. "Your brother had heart troubles," I said.

He nodded. "My brother had a heart attack at age 43."

"Mike, your brother wants you to know that your parents were there to greet him when he passed."

Mike had always hoped that his brother wasn't alone, so just hearing those words put some of his own fears to rest.

"Who's the coin collector?" I asked. "Is there someone who would hoard spare change?"

Mike started to laugh. "That was my mother. She collected little packets of coins until they filled an entire coffee can. Then she'd take them to the bank and put the extra money in her savings account."

"And she didn't like to spend any of it, did she?"

"No," Mike admitted. "It almost made her physically ill to spend a dollar. She was a big saver."

"I've got your father here, too." As I reached down, I felt air below my leg. "He lost his leg, right?"

"That's right," Mike said in an amazed voice. "He had the lower part of his leg amputated below the knee."

"Your father also says that he's sorry about the drinking while he was here." Acknowledging that this was a painful part of his past with a somber nod, Mike looked as if he was ready for me to move on. I paused for a moment as I quickly saw the state of Tennessee in my mind. "Who's going to Memphis or somewhere else in Tennessee soon?"

Mike started to shake his head. "My wife and I are going there in a few weeks for business," he said, dropping his program for the evening because he couldn't quite believe what was happening.

"Your father really likes your new boat. He thinks that you should keep it docked by the house."

Mike laughed, because he was trying to decide where to keep his new toy.

"He's also sending his love to your kids and thanks you for naming one of the boys after him."

Mike's eyes now welled with tears.

"He was in the military, correct? I want to call him 'sir.'" I could see from the look on Mike's face that I was correct, so I continued. "And I know he wasn't around a lot when you were younger. Your mom had the difficult job of raising you by herself, which your dad will appreciate for eternity because she did such a fine job. Your father also wants to say that he really likes your wife, and you're a lucky man to have her in your life."

Sheryl piped up and said, "I think Mike's pop is absolutely correct!"

The crowd burst into laughter and applause, but suddenly I heard a softer voice. I said, "Mike, your mom is coming through now, but she had to let your father have his say first. She's telling me that she'll always be with you, and that both of them will be at the wedding next year. Do you understand that?"

"Yes, my daughter is getting married next year," Mike replied.

"Your mom keeps bringing me to February of next year. I don't know what's happening, but keep an eye on that date," I said.

His father suddenly came back and had one final message to give Mike. "Your father says, 'Take care of your health. I'll watch over the grandchildren, and I'll see you again one day.'"

Everyone hoped that it would be a long, long time before the two made that connection again, but Mike had some frightening health concerns to face—his entire family had a history of heart disease. After our reading, Mike told me that he'd just recovered from a mild heart attack months before the cruise, but he was keeping a close check on his health.

As I was writing this book, I sadly found out that Mike had passed from a massive heart attack just a few days before February 14, when, coincidentally, he was scheduled to do another psychic healing cruise. In fact, during the last year of his life, Mike became almost obsessed with investigating the afterlife, which proves to me that somehow his spirit was preparing him to cross. An angel, in the form of his mother, was right about watching that February date, and I know she was the one to greet him when he crossed over.

In her grief, Sheryl was comforted by the fact that she knew Mike was with his father and mother again. And she knew that she'd see him again when the time was right. She wasn't alone, and was comforted by the memory that most days with Mike were like Valentine's Day.

Since then, Sheryl has told me that Mike has contacted her, and I can report that he's a clever spirit. Here's a perfect example from Sheryl: "When he was alive, Mike always said, 'Sheryl, if I die, we should have a code so I can reach you from the Other Side.' I always said, 'I don't want to talk about this stuff.' But one thing we used to say to each other all the time after a fight was, 'I love you, even though you're a pain in the ass.'

"Not long ago, I found those words written on the top of my checkbook register," an amazed Sheryl told me, adding, "And then, a few days later, I met a woman who had also lost her husband. She told me that her husband always used to tell her, 'I love you even if you're a pain in the ass.'"

"It was as if Mike was sending a message," Sheryl concluded. "John, you gave me the peace to know that Mike is healthy on the Other Side and he's with his family who's taking care of him. That was always my job. So as long as I know that someone's doing that, I can go on until I see my beloved again."

— ◎ —

chapter 11

OUR CHILDREN

THE LOVE BETWEEN A PARENT and child is one of the most precious and deep connections we make during our time on Earth. Children start out as part of us, and from their first cries of hello, they establish themselves as the biggest part of our hearts. We dream of watching our kids grow up, stand on their own, and run free because it's the natural order of things. Of course, a parent wants to leave the planet before their son or daughter makes that final journey—and sometimes we can't understand why life doesn't cooperate and a child is taken to the Other Side.

When this happens, a parent is left with more questions than answers: *Why did this happen? Is the universe a fair place? Who's taking care of my child now?*

Sadly, no one seems to want to talk about the death of a child because they fear it will make the suffering parent feel even more uncomfortable. That's why many who have suffered this loss decide to seek out a medium to assist in their bereavement process.

Reading for parents who have lost children is very special to me and always strokes my heart. The following stories stick out in my mind, as they show the powerful connection between parents and the children who have gone on before them.

Spirit Needs No Address

On the cruise I mentioned in the previous chapter, my attention was immediately drawn to the couple sitting beside Mike and Sheryl. "I'm hearing the name Ron. I believe he's somebody who passed really young and quickly."

"I had a young son who passed quickly. His name was Ron, Jr., and I'm Ron, Sr.," said the middle-aged man sitting before me. It turns out that Ron, Jr., had passed a few years earlier in an automobile accident. At age 17, he was out one night riding around in his Mustang, lost control of the car, and crashed into a clump of trees.

"Your boy wants you to know that his passing was fast and he felt no pain. He wants to thank you for your prayers," I told him. "Ron, Jr., was a very sensitive and emotional boy. In fact, I can feel the softness of his energy now. He truly is an angel. But what's with his neck?" I asked as I rubbed my own neck.

"My son died when he broke his neck," Ron said, sobbing a bit even though he could usually control such outbursts in the presence of other people.

"Ron, your son doesn't hurt anymore. In fact, the accident happened so fast that he didn't feel a thing," I said in a soft voice, hoping that I was alleviating some of his pain.

The boy had been gone for three years, and during that time his father never had never gotten answers to the questions that kept him awake at night. Although I'd put some of his fears to rest, he still had some other concerns. "My biggest worry is that we moved, and now we're away from his grave," he finally admitted.

This wasn't a tough one for me, but I turned to Ron, Jr., who provided me with the necessary information. "Young Ronnie knows you're in Florida, and he can find you there," I told his parents, adding, "Of course, you know he's not really in there. The graves are basically for *us*—they're just places we go because that's where we think they are. Spirit isn't confined to one particular space or state, or any of the confines of geography for that matter.

"Spirit is everywhere," I continued. "Right now, Ronnie's spirit is here, and he's thanking you for the memorial. However, I feel like there was more than one celebration of his life. Do you understand that?"

Ron nodded and said, "The first thing we did in his memory was to collect money to help other kids who were hurt in car accidents. And the second memorial is one that the high school built—a special trophy case with a plaque at the bottom that reads: *In loving memory of Ronnie.*"

"He must have been pretty good at sports, because he's showing me his letterman's jacket. He's also talking to me about a ring."

"I do have his jacket and his senior ring," said Ron, Sr.

"He wants you to wear them both. Those are for you, Dad, because the two of you enjoyed sports so much together. You and he must have loved baseball, because I see a bat. He still wants you to go and enjoy the game yourself."

By now, Ron was openly weeping, but I pressed on. "Wow—for someone who was a shy boy, Ronnie's having no problem talking to me now," I said. "In fact, now he's playing me a little song and laughing, too. I even hear a guitar." I started to strum with one hand.

"He was always playing the guitar," said his father, actually laughing a little bit now at the memory.

I continued to strum and told the audience that Ron, Jr., was still playing his tunes. "He's playing now, and he's not half bad," I said. To his parents, I said, "Ronnie also wants you to know that he'll keep coming to you when you need him."

The information that came through put Ron's mind at ease. His son had passed so young that he needed to know that Ronnie was fine, happy, and not alone. This emotional father also wanted to be able to find his namesake when he needed him. As he said later, "It was very comforting to me to know that my boy is still here in spirit, and he's never far away."

The Pink Princess

Victoria was a lovely 50-year-old woman whom I also met on the cruise. She hailed from the Napa Valley, where she ran a quaint trinket shop. It was obvious that she was alone on the cruise, and she was exceptionally sad.

Right away, I started to link with a spirit. I asked, "Who's known for being an artist in the family? I have someone who's passed who was truly a great painter."

"Why, my sister Judy was an artist who loved to paint," Victoria replied.

"I also have your mom and dad here. They've been gone a long time."

Victoria began to smile.

"Mom and Dad want me to tell you that they're here for you—and they're here with someone else who's very special to you," I said.

Victoria sat so still that she looked like a statue. She'd attended this cruise hoping that it would provide some sort of comfort after a year of mourning, and it seems that she was going to get her wish.

"I see a young girl who passed quickly—very quickly," I continued. "In fact, she was moving at great speeds when she passed, but it wasn't in a car. It was such a strange accident that it was in many newspapers." At this point, I felt an odd stirring. "She hit her back, right?"

Victoria nodded, the sadness now consuming her face. Her sorrow had been mostly a private affair, and she'd spent much of the past year crying, screaming, and looking up into the sky for answers. "My daughter died last year," she finally whispered, and looked away sadly.

"Whose birthday cake am I seeing? I see the number 22," I said.

"She would have been 18 on the 22nd," Victoria said, composing herself.

At that point, I knew that I'd found the biggest chunk of information that would certainly convince Victoria that the spirit of her daughter was here. "She died in the water and was moving very fast," I told her. "And now I feel tingling in both my back and neck. What's happening here?"

It was then that Victoria told me that the light of her life, her daughter, Quimby (Swedish for "life saving"), passed away on a school field trip to a local amusement park. The honor-roll student was looking forward to graduation and starting college in the fall. She knew that her entire life was ahead of her, so it was time to just blow off some steam, which coincided in the happiest way with the field trip. Quimby and her friends always loved the water rides, and since this was a hot California day, they chose to go down a massive slide, which was supposed to toss riders into a huge pool.

Unfortunately, the girls wouldn't reach the water safely. In a horrendous accident, the slide snapped in two while they were rushing down it, at speeds of up to 70 miles an hour. Quimby was the only one who was killed that day, although many of her classmates were in critical condition for months.

"She was a princess—*your* princess. And for some reason, she's surrounding herself with the color pink," I told Victoria. I stopped for a minute to listen to Quimby's spirit before I said to her mother, "I keep hearing the name 'Girly Girl.' What's that all about?"

"My daughter liked pink frilly stuff. She was very feminine, and it was a wonderful part of her personality. So I called her Girly Girl. She'd sign her notes to me, 'Love, your Girly Girl,'" Victoria said, fighting back the tears.

"Victoria, your daughter wants you to know that she's not in any pain. She didn't even know what was happening during the accident. It happened so quickly that she didn't feel any of it. She also wants you to know that she's been sending you warm greetings because you don't like to . . . what does this mean? You don't like to turn on the heat?"

With that, Victoria actually laughed because she knew exactly what I meant. "The one and only thing my daughter and I ever fought over was the fact that I refused to turn on the heat until November 1. I wanted to save money on the bills because I was a single mother. Well, Quimby was always freezing in September, so she'd try to sneak downstairs and turn it on. When I'd turn it back off, she'd walk around the house in her winter coat as a protest. Last September after she passed, I came downstairs on the first chilly morning, and the heat was on. I live alone, and I know *I* didn't turn it on."

"Mom, your Girly Girl is laughing now, and she wants you to be happy. She wants to give you a hug and tell you that's she's fine. Quimby also wants you to inform your ex-husband that she'll visit him, too, when his cold gets better."

Victoria was astounded. "He always did get colds this time of year."

"Most of all, Mom, Quimby is so proud of how you're trying to help other kids avoid getting hurt at amusement parks." It turns out that after Quimby's death, Victoria began spending several days a week donating her time to hospices and also working to pass stricter safety laws when it comes to aging amusement parks and their dangerous rides. "Quimby says, 'Way to go, Mom,' and keep up the good work because everyone deserves a mother just like you. She feels lucky that of all the moms in the universe, she got the best one possible. And she also says that you should start writing your book. Do it now," I said. "Your daughter says so."

It was true that Victoria had always planned to write a book, but in her grief over her daughter's death, she felt paralyzed. "Now knowing that Quimby is safe and her spirit lives on, I can go on," she said through her tears. "I'll do it for my Girly Girl."

The Four Angels

There's an old saying about finding strength in numbers, and perhaps that's why many people choose to see me in a group setting. It's almost as if the sheer presence of other people provides a safety net: If I happen to link with one person's relatives, the kind wishes of those around them seem to elevate the mood. Everyone can share in the experience in that way.

Two smartly dressed ladies named Barbara and Claire convinced each other that it might be worth coming to one of my group sessions in Boston. Claire even went one step further—she dragged along Darryl, her skeptical husband, who had never been exposed to any type of mediumship demonstration, claiming that he didn't believe in this sort of thing.

As Claire insisted later, "My husband was very skeptical about going to see a medium, but I begged him to come with me. I knew that if John somehow gave some evidence about our loss, then I wanted Darryl by my side. He needed to know, too."

Of course, I didn't know about any of these private discussions and just approached the group of ten like any other session. Just as I do with every group, I told everyone what to expect, informing them how the spirits would come through and how my mediumship works. After cautioning them not to feed me any information, I asked them to let the spirits do their job. Finally, I said, "Just let go of your expectations." Silently, I said a prayer, which is something I always do before a group begins.

On this night, I found myself linking with a spirit who was definitely male and someone's brother. "Who in the group understands losing a brother?"

What I didn't see from the front of the room was Claire gently nudging Darryl, who had buried his brother 13 years previously. Darryl's hand didn't go up; in fact, he sat with his arms crossed over his chest. He was a bit closed off to the entire process, to say the least.

I went on: "Now, I feel like this brother figure possibly passed from a motorcycle accident."

Claire frantically pulled on the shirt of her friend Barbara because she knew that this was exactly how her brother-in-law had passed. Then Claire began to stare at her husband, who reluctantly raised his hand.

"Your brother is the one who wants credit for opening the door this evening," I told him. "He wants you to know that he's here and he's bringing someone very precious with him—someone much younger." I paused for a moment when the vision of a young woman with long, flowing brown hair came to me. "Is this your daughter?"

Claire looked shocked, and her husband grasped her hand.

"This was a fast passing, correct?" I asked them.

"Yes," they said in one voice.

"I feel that this happened in an automobile accident, and she wasn't alone when she passed. I see three other girls in a car with her. In fact, one of the other girl's mothers is here tonight with you, Claire."

At that point, Barbara let out a tiny sob and grasped Claire's other hand.

Claire replied, "John, both Barbara and I lost our beautiful daughters . . . and they were so young. We lost them in a horrible auto accident." She couldn't speak any longer, and Barbara apologized, too, because she needed a moment to pull herself together.

"Take all the time you need," I said. "Claire, I see a beautiful young girl in front of me who keeps twisting her long brown hair in her fingers. She's even flipping it over her head. I see her sitting at a table and . . . she must really love that hair because now she's running her fingers through it."

Claire and her husband looked at each other and shared a knowing laugh. "That's our Vickie. Her hair truly was her crowning glory."

"I also have another girl here tonight with Vickie who seems a little more quiet. It seems that Vickie's the outspoken one. But the other girl wants to say hello to her mother." I kept hearing a *D* name in my head, but it wasn't an average one. "The other girl's name begins with a *D*. Not Donna or Diane, it's something a bit more unusual," I said.

"That's my Diedra!" Barbara exclaimed.

"Vickie's jumping up and down with excitement. She's sending a lot of love to her parents. Your daughter also wants you to know that she was with your grandson in the hospital. Something was wrong with . . . his stomach. Is that right?"

"Yes," Claire confirmed. "My newborn grandson, Xander, had a malformation in his stomach that they discovered right after birth—he just had a major operation to correct it."

"Vickie wants you to know that the baby is going to be okay and will grow up to be strong and healthy." I paused for a moment. "Can this be right? She knows that he'll speak three languages."

By this time, Claire was laughing. "We're French. My son married a Chinese woman and, of course, the baby will speak English. Three languages!" she said.

I turned to Barbara. "Now your daughter is jumping in. Diedra wants to put your fears to rest. She knows that you're still so worried that she suffered during the accident. There was no pain, Mom." I looked directly into her eyes. "The fire doesn't matter anymore. Your girls were beautiful here, and they're beautiful now."

Claire and Barbara filled me in on what all of this meant. In 1998, Vickie, Diedra, and two girlfriends had come home for a break after their first semester of college. The mothers wanted to drive their daughters back to school, but the girls insisted that wasn't necessary. Vickie would take her trusty old car and drive the girls back to their dorms. And so, the moms kissed their girls good-bye for the last time.

On the way back to school, a young man saw the four beautiful girls and started honking and calling out to them on the highway. It escalated to where he'd pass the girls' tiny economy car, stopping short and then letting them get ahead of him—a very dangerous highway game.

Unfortunately, this man miscalculated on one of his last cat-and-mouse maneuvers. Vickie tried to speed up and lose him, but she wound up losing control of the car, which was now going dangerously fast. Suddenly, she saw a large snow-plow swing across the highway dividing line. The snow-plow hit the girls' car hard, and the little vehicle immediately burst into flames. Sadly, there were no survivors.

"Claire and Barbara, both of your girls want you to know that they're together on the Other Side," I said. "They're still best friends, and they're happy. Most of all, they want their parents to let go of their blame and guilt. It was no one's fault—it was an accident. And there was no way that they were going to allow you to drive them back to school.

"These are really strong, independent girls," I told them. "They're also very involved in your lives. Vickie was there when your grandson was born, Claire. She was right there in the delivery room. Now she's telling me, 'You've made our dream come true for the other children. Way to go, Mom.'"

It seems that before the tragedy, Vickie and Claire were working on opening a home day-care center as partners. But after losing her daughter, Claire thought about scrapping the plans because it was just too painful to go it alone. Yet she persevered. "I knew my daughter would want me to be surrounded with children, so I pushed on and opened the center," Claire said.

"Vickie makes regular visits to the day-care center and sometimes works right beside you, Claire, just like you planned it," I told her.

At this point, Claire rested her head on her husband's shoulder.

"Diedra wants to thank everyone for the angels. The angel statue, more specifically," I said. "Do you know what this means?"

Barbara and Claire linked hands again and smiled widely—they knew exactly what this meant. After losing four bright young girls, their town decided that the best honor would be to erect a large brick structure in the public park with a clock on top of it and a bench underneath as a peaceful resting spot for everyone. On the ground is a bronze plaque with four angels on it and a heart in the middle. On the bottom is the inscription: *Forever in Our Hearts, Forever in God's Hands.*

"They love that no one has forgotten them," I said.

"I even named our day-care center 'Angels of Mine,'" Claire interjected.

"Those girls *are* our angels," said Barbara. "And now I feel blessed because I always thought I had someone looking over my shoulder. Now I know that I have four angels with me."

At that moment, I heard a new spirit voice coming through, and I knew it was another one of the girls, but sadly her mom wasn't in the group that evening. "I have a message for another mom whose daughter's name begins with a *K*," I said. "Who has the *K* name? This girl also wants to say hello and that she's fine."

"That's Kristen," Claire gasped. "I'll make sure to tell her mother the minute we get home."

I had another question. "Did one of the girls do something to give you a sign—to make her presence known? Something about a photo of someone also associated with angels?"

At this point, Claire gasped. She explained that when her grandson was born, the family took a snapshot of him in his crib. What came back from the photo developers was very strange indeed: In the snapshot, the baby is in the middle with two shadows on either side of him that look like the shapes of angels. There was also a faint outline of a heart in the middle.

"I always knew it. I always just knew," Claire said softly.

"Now you don't have to wonder, Mom. It was just Aunt Vickie saying hello to her new nephew."

Look Ma, No Wheels!

They arrived as a family, and their presence proved to me that my readings are often for many ears to hear. Once a spirit has an open line to this world, it often wants several listeners on the other end. That was the case with Denise and Kathy, sisters from Massachusetts who decided one spring morning that it was a beautiful day to take a drive out to see me. It was Denise who had arranged for the reading, so her sister sat quietly in my waiting room.

I said hello to Kathy on my way upstairs to see Denise, and thought that would be our only greeting. Later, I had to laugh because even when I make plans, I have to remind myself that I'm not always in control of the reading . . . but let's not get too far ahead just yet. Kathy stayed downstairs in my waiting room while Denise, a bright career woman in her 40s, met with me to settle some issues that were keeping her awake at night.

Almost immediately, we got right down to work. "Denise, your mom has passed. She's right here beside you, and there's a lot of love coming from her."

Denise began nodding her head, and I could see the tension leaving her face as if someone was wiping it away.

I continued on. "Your mom says that she knows you were the one who was really there for her during her final days, although she certainly doesn't blame anyone else in the family for not being there. She just loves and thanks you for taking on most of the responsibility. As usual, you were her 'strong girl.'"

One of three sisters, Denise was the closest and most available to her mother who had suffered from heart and kidney problems. During her last days in the hospital, it was Denise who staged round-the-clock vigils, sitting by her mother's bedside and just holding her hand while repeating, "Everything's going to be fine. We love you. Please hang on." It turns out that hanging on wasn't going to be easy because basically all of her mother's organs were shutting down, and doctors said it was "just a matter of time" before she passed on. Many families would give up at this point, but not Denise.

I noticed the sweet smell of lavender. "Did you rub special cream on your mother while she was ill?" Denise whispered yes.

"Mom wants to thank you for going to the hospital and rubbing her legs with that cream that felt so good. She says to stop beating yourself up for missing one night of visiting her. Even *she* knew you had other responsibilities. She also wants me to thank you for riding in the ambulance to the hospital with her because it made her feel so much calmer. She felt you stroking her hair, even when the doctors told you that she was in a coma and couldn't feel or understand a thing. She felt your hand, and it made her feel better. She heard your words," I told her.

Then the mood switched because Denise's mom didn't want to dwell on the sad times anymore. "Bingo! Bingo! Bingo! Why is your mom screaming that to me?"

Denise began to giggle, telling me that her mom's favorite thing in the world was to play bingo. In fact, she was a bit of an addict.

"Did you put something in the casket? Your mom is thanking you for it."

"When Mom died, I snuck a little bingo marker in her casket!" Denise explained, laughing harder.

"I think she's playing a few games over there." I smiled. "There's also someone there with her who's younger. Do you know a Johnny?"

Denise tried to swallow fresh tears, but they flowed down her cheeks.

"Why is he saying that he's running like the wind, and no one can stop him now?" I asked. "What does this mean to you, Denise?"

By now, Denise was noticeably amazed, and even I felt a little tingle of excitement because it was clear that this wasn't an average reading. "John," she said, "the boy is my nephew. He's the son of my sister who's sitting downstairs."

At that moment, I knew what we had to do. "Let me go get her—her son wants to talk to her."

All at once, I ran downstairs at a speed that might qualify me for the Olympics. By the time I hit my waiting room, I found a sleepy Kathy relaxing in the warmth of the sunlight that was coming in through the windows.

"Kathy," I said, startling her, "I'm sorry to surprise you this way, but could you come upstairs for a minute? There's someone who wants to talk to you."

"My sister?" she asked.

"No," I said, gently. "Your son."

Kathy looked a bit dazed, but she followed me upstairs and sat next to her sister on the couch. Without even being aware of it, the women held hands.

"Kathy, Johnny says he wants me to tell you that he's playing baseball. He's running the bases all by himself," I said. "He doesn't need his helpers anymore."

"Oh my God, oh my God!" Kathy said over and over again. "No helpers?" she repeated.

"No—he's says that he's standing tall," I said.

When she could compose herself, Kathy filled me in. "Johnny was born with spina bifida and spent his entire life in a wheelchair. His younger sister, who's 12 now, has muscular dystrophy, and she's also spent her life in a wheelchair. "

"For a little kid, Johnny's presence is really strong," I told her. "He told me to get you because he has a lot to say. First, he doesn't want you to blame anyone for his accident."

Johnny died in 1992 at the age of nine. Ironically, he was in the best health of his life. In fact, he was feeling so good that the family decided that it was time for him to go to school by himself. Although his body had limitations, he was, by all accounts, a smart, savvy boy who liked to learn; and he loved the company of other children.

But one horrible morning, an inexperienced bus driver failed to secure his wheelchair into the slots of a special van that took Johnny to school. When the driver hit the gas, the unlocked wheels of the chair lurched back, and Johnny's head snapped back hard. The driver didn't notice, and Johnny was deprived of oxygen for too long, lapsing him into a two-day coma that ended with his death.

Almost a decade had passed since then, and it was clear to me that he had quite a lot to say to the mother he still adored. "Besides being a very smart kid, he must have had a lot of energy, because he's all over the room now," I told a now-smiling Kathy. "He loved the fact that you didn't treat him like he was different, and you allowed him to fly when he was on Earth. In fact, he wants me to remind you about the day he rode in the fire truck."

"That's something only Johnny and I knew!" Kathy said. "During an inspection of our home, one of the firemen asked Johnny if he wanted to go around the block in the truck. I wasn't sure if the entire family would approve, but I had to give him a chance to live like a normal boy, so I said okay."

"Mom, he says it was the best day of his life," I told her before I shifted gears. "Who sleeps to the music?"

"My daughter listens to classical music every night because it soothes her," Kathy said.

"Johnny listens with her, and he's also helping her to sleep quietly through the night," I told Kathy. While she wrapped her mind around that, I nodded to my left. But I wasn't sure if I should say the next bit of information that Johnny was telling me. "Kathy, Johnny says that he's with his other siblings."

Kathy gasped. "I had three miscarriages before Johnny," she whispered. "But I never thought of them as 'whole' children because they weren't born."

"Even if a child never makes it to Earth, they still go back into the spirit world and continue to grow as children. Johnny's saying he's with his family," I told her. And now I was about to dispense another bit of news that I thought she might find a bit eye-opening. "Even though I know he passed as a child, I feel him as much older. Johnny wants you to know that he's not a little boy anymore. He doesn't want to be called a baby." And to him, I said, "I know, I know, Johnny, you're a big guy now."

"He never wanted to be treated like a baby," Kathy said.

"No, it's not just that—he really wants you to feel like he's a grown-up. He actually *has* matured and grown up on the Other Side," I told her. "He wants you to know that he no longer needs the wheelchair. And he wants me to say these words to you: 'Look, Ma, no wheels! I'm as free as a butterfly.'"

I explained to Kathy and Denise that no one is ever handicapped when they cross over, for all their physical problems are suddenly gone.

Kathy began to openly weep and, very softly, I passed on another message: "He thanks you for that special tombstone you created for him because it came true."

After many tissues, Kathy finally said, "On his grave-stone, we have an etching of a wheelchair, but Johnny's not in it—he's walking toward God with outstretched arms. The chair is far behind him because he doesn't need it anymore."

I smiled. "Johnny also wants you to know that he's there with your mother, your grandmother, and your husband's parents. Who has the *J* name?"

"My husband's sister, Janey, passed a few years ago," Kathy said.

"Tell your husband that Janey came through. Plus, your mom wants you to know that she'll always watch over Johnny."

"Why is someone is calling out 'Dumbo'?" I inquired. "Is this the family pet?"

Both Kathy and Denise started to laugh. "No, John, it's my son again," Kathy said. "When I was a kid, I had big ears, and Johnny inherited them. So we called ourselves 'the Dum-bos.' It was our own private joke."

By this time, Johnny's energy was fading a bit, and I looked back at Denise. Of course she was thrilled that Kathy could finally communicate with her son and didn't wish for one minute that the session had gone any differently. But an hour had passed, and she was standing up, knowing that our time was almost over.

"Denise, could you please sit down?" I asked. "I have one more person who needs to say hello to you before you leave. Who's Michael?"

As her hand flew to her mouth, Denise leaned back down on the couch for support.

"Michael says that he knows you miss him. You are and always will be his number-one girl," I told her.

Denise said, "Michael was the boy I loved in high school. Even though we were only 17, I thought that I'd marry him— "

I finished for her. "But he died quickly in a car accident."

"He loved to speed around town in this car that he had rebuilt and was so proud of," Denise said. "I remember the day they made the announcement at school that he'd died. I had to be sent home because I couldn't believe it had happened."

"Can this be right? He's telling me that you talk to him in the shower?" I asked.

Denise squirmed in her seat, and I could see her blush, as if this was one of those secrets she didn't want revealed. Slowly, she admitted, "I *do* talk to Michael from time to time. I've even told my husband about it, and it doesn't bother him," Denise said. "I've always felt silly about this, but, yes, if I'm missing Michael and I want to talk to him, I'll chat with him when I'm in the shower."

"He wants you to know that he met someone very special where he is now, and the two of them like to toss the baseball around together. He's friends with your nephew Johnny, and they're hanging out together," I said.

Kathy had to smile, because when she was a young girl, she was always fond of Michael. It made her happy that he was now Johnny's "big brother" on the Other Side.

I had one more thing to tell her: "Hey Mom, right now Johnny says he's running the bases and he just made it home."

Chrissy

Most of the time, the spirits will confine themselves to my left side, but in some circumstances they can envelop the space around me, a floor of my house, or even the entire building. People who claim to have no psychic or intuitive abilities have witnessed this extraordinary phenomenon happening in my home, which I call a psychic "rub-off."

This happened during a really busy period in my life when I was trying to see as many clients as possible at my home in Cambridge. On this particular midwinter's night, the temperatures hovered below zero, and I was busy heating up my reading room to make it comfortable for my next client.

I'd already read for two women that night, but I knew that I only had to see one more client before turning in for the day. All I knew was that my next appointment was with Linda, a woman in her early 40s, whose husband, Richard, refused to sit with her—he wanted to drop her off and then wait in the car for an hour for her to return. As soon as I heard that this was the plan, I protested because he'd freeze out there. I told Richard to just wait in my living room, where he could watch some TV, read a few magazines, and relax.

With Linda's husband's happily watching the evening news and avoiding frostbite, I made a last-minute check of the surroundings to make sure everything was ready. To my delight, the house was almost completely still, as if the hustle and bustle outside had been suspended in time. The phone wasn't ringing, sirens weren't blaring—my surroundings were calm, peaceful, and perfect.

Linda looked hopeful when I led her to my private reading room where I allowed her a few minutes to settle in and get acclimated before I returned to start the reading. (I always give clients this private time to relax and calm down.)

I went to get us two glasses of water and glanced at the clock, realizing that it was seven o'clock on the dot. This meant that my friend Simon, who was visiting me from England, would soon be home from his day on the town. It dawned on me at that moment that I'd forgotten to warn him that half of this couple was waiting in my living room, but it was too late—Simon had returned. He was used to my clients coming and going each night, and although he'd always say a polite hello, he rarely hung around them. To put it bluntly, this was not his "thing," and I certainly didn't expect him to talk to everyone who came for a reading. That was *my* job!

Little did I know that something incredible would happen on this evening—not just in my reading room, but also between Simon and the woman's husband. . . .

I returned to Linda, who had settled down and was ready to begin her reading. Immediately, I linked with a little girl, and I sensed that she'd passed away less than a year ago. I looked across at Linda and decided to go slow before I gave her the evidence presented to me.

"Linda, did you lose a daughter?"

"Yes," she sadly replied.

"Well, your daughter wastes no time—she's right here and ready to get to work!" I told her. I was only sensing the little girl, not getting any direct messages that I could translate into words. However, the little girl was so excited to be here that I could feel her giddiness and enthusiasm.

Linda looked down, and I could see the tears trickling down her face.

"She keeps showing me a *C*, but I can't hear her. It's like she's drawing the letter *C* with her finger," I said, turning my head to the left as I strained to listen more closely.

"John, her name is Chrissy."

"You know, Linda, I've been doing this work for a while, but your little girl appears to be communicating with pictures rather than words. I'm clairaudient, and I usually always get words, but in this case, it's all coming through as images and feelings. I don't understand."

"That would figure," Linda replied softly, still not looking up. "My daughter was mute and couldn't speak."

I told her that when we pass to the Other Side, we get *all* our faculties back, including those we may never have had during this lifetime. But I finally figured out that Chrissy was communicating this way to make sure that her mom knew it was definitely her.

"Linda, she must be a good artist—I like what I'm seeing and how she's getting it across to me."

"Yes, she was great at painting and drawing."

"She's mentioning her brother, who's close to her in age." I could feel Chrissy's excitement grow even stronger for a second, and realized that these two children must have had a strong bond.

"Yes, she has a brother, and she adored him."

"Something must have happened while you were having her. I feel as though she was underdeveloped and probably mentally challenged." As I was talking, I realized that something serious must have happened and that this child had lived her short life with enormous difficulties and many medical obstacles to overcome. I could see frequent visits to the hospital and doctors around her all through her life.

Linda broke in to confirm, telling me, "There were complications in the delivery room that left her with neurological disorders. She passed when she was 16, but she really had the mind of a 10-year-old."

"She wants to send love to Daddy and her brother. Please tell them that she's okay now. She's not alone. I feel a grandmother figure who's now taking care of Chrissy." I paused because the little girl wanted to tell me something that was troubling her. With great care, I told Linda the following: "Chrissy's concerned that you and your husband have drifted apart, and she says it's time for the two of you now. She knows everything you did for her, and she feels that you were the best parents ever."

Linda started to weep and told me that she and her husband had forgotten how to be a couple. After Chrissy's death, it was almost as if they didn't know each other anymore. Meanwhile, as her mother talked about how she feared for her marriage, Chrissy continued to come through with more evidence. She kept showing me images and scenes from her own private movies of her parents kissing, hugging, and holding hands—little gestures of kindness over the years. She was persistent and kept coming back to the same subject over and over again. She wanted to see her mom and dad back together again as a loving couple. This was an extraordinary demonstration of love, and I was in awe of this little girl and her determination.

Some 70 minutes later, Linda and I hugged and agreed that this was an amazing, eye-opening night. She vowed to concentrate as hard as possible when it came to mending her marriage, because it wasn't just what *she* wanted—it was also the wish of her beautiful daughter.

Still drying her tears, Linda accompanied me downstairs to find her husband and fill him in on what had happened. A few stairs from the bottom, I glanced into the living room and saw Simon and Richard facing each other on opposite sofas. The room was dim, but even so, I noticed that both men had strange looks on their faces. At that moment, Richard looked up and saw Linda, noticing her tear-streaked face.

I broke the silence. "So, what have you two been talking about for all this time?" I thought they might say the news or sports, but that wasn't even close to the truth.

Simon said, "I'm not sure why, but tonight I felt the need to sit and talk to Richard. Now, John, you know that I normally prefer to eat early, but tonight I just felt compelled to sit here. The minute I began talking to him, it was like winter had crept into the house. Both of us kept feeling this cold draft brush over our legs, and I even felt it pass through my body. It was so strong that it made my back arch." He added, "I also kept hearing a voice in my head, and it was as though I was being told to pass a message on to Richard."

"What was it?" I asked.

Simon replied, "The voice said, 'Tell him he needs to court his wife again.' That's what I heard over and over again. It sounded stupid to me at first because why should I tell this complete stranger—a married man—to court his wife? Yet I saw in my mind, as clear as a day, this image of Richard walking up his front path with flowers, ringing their doorbell, and then asking his wife out on a date. Is that crazy or what?"

Of course, I knew it wasn't crazy at all. His story had an uncanny similarity with the reading I'd just given upstairs.

Simon continued. "What's even stranger is that it wasn't my voice I heard. I felt it come from an older woman with snow-white hair who was here with us, right in this room!"

By now, he was talking very fast, as though it was important for him to get his story out as quickly as possible. I'd never seen Simon like this before, and I noticed him shiver again while he was speaking. "I kept hearing the letter *E* in my head," he said. "Over and over again, I heard the voice saying, 'Tell him *E, E, E.*'" He said that he and Richard had even heard a voice coming from the corner of the room, but they couldn't understand what she was saying. "I checked around—no one else was in the house," Simon said in a shaky voice before adding, "What the bloody hell is going on?"

Richard had been sitting quietly as Simon spoke. I could tell that he was a little shaken, too, because he struggled to form the words as he slowly explained that his grandmother's name was Edie. She'd been very close to him, and he often felt her energy around him. "It was a tragedy when I lost her," he said in a quivering tone.

Richard and Linda sat close to each other and filled us in on some of the more personal details of their lives. For 16 years, they'd cared for their little girl, providing a home to cater to her special needs. Sacrificing their lives and even their marriage, they always slept with their daughter between them because one of them needed to be able to resuscitate her when she stopped breathing during the night. Both had refused to put their daughter in a special home, choosing to take care of her themselves so that she'd feel safe.

Tears formed in my eyes as I listened to them, and I felt privileged that Richard and Linda had chosen to share their story with me. In the next few moments, I learned that they'd buried Chrissy a year before coming to see me, but clearly the time since her passing had taken its toll on both of them. Yet as they sat there together, I noticed that they were holding hands.

"We've been talking about needing something to reconnect us. We were desperate to find each other again," Richard said.

Needless to say, it was a special night—one I'll never forget. This couple closed one door and opened another, right before my very eyes. At the time, I decided that I had the most rewarding job on Earth.

As they drove away, I turned and faced my English friend. "Now, Simon, I want to know what's going on with *you?* Are you a medium, too?"

He could only release a nervous laugh because he was a bit confused by the whole experience. Who wouldn't be a bit startled? For a man who didn't find the spirit world his "thing," it was a bit of a mind-blowing evening to say the least.

Now, just in case you're wondering what was going on that evening, let me explain it in the simplest way possible. Apparently, Chrissy had met up with her great-grandmother— both of whom were concerned about Linda and Richard's relationship and wanted to help. With a team like that working for them, I can only assume that Richard and Linda *did* find each other again, and Chrissy's very proud that she helped make it all possible.

As always, the spirit world never ceases to amaze me!

Heaven's Little Dancer

During her time on Earth, she was often called "a little butterfly angel." Jennifer had such a spark inside of her that the five-year-old seemed to be illuminated from the inside out, and her spirit couldn't be kept still. This kid wanted to fly. Of course, I didn't know anything about this special little girl until I "met" her during an appointment with her mother, Melinda, a hospital worker from California.

For more than a year, Melinda had been thinking about consulting a medium, and then she heard about me from a friend when I lived in Los Angeles. "In my mind, I thought I was having visions of my little girl, but I couldn't be sure," she says now. "Was I losing my mind? I needed someone I could trust to tell me how I could find something so precious that I refused to believe was lost forever."

Our meeting actually began during a brief conversation that I felt compelled to have with Melinda before we shook hands. Usually, I had an assistant set up the appointments, but something was telling me to call this woman myself—someone was actually insisting that I do so.

About one minute into our brief introduction via the telephone, I saw a little girl who had only been gone for a short time. "Melinda, did you lose a daughter?" I asked her.

The sharp intake of breath was my answer.

"She's standing over her brother," I continued. "She just loves him so much."

As I said this, Melinda told me that she glanced next to her where her son was quietly playing.

A month later, I had the pleasure of meeting Melinda. We sat down in my office, and suddenly I felt a link to an elderly man with a warm face full of laugh lines. "Melinda, I think I have your grandfather here, and he's standing with someone hiding behind his leg. In fact, she loves to play hide-and-seek." I smiled because I knew it had to be the little girl again. "She's telling me that her name begins with a *J*."

Melinda confirmed that her beloved daughter's name was Jennifer. Next, I heard the *clackity-clackity-clack* sound that I described in the introduction of this book. If you recall, I thought that Jennifer liked to tap dance, but her mother simply laughed, wiped away a couple of tears, and explained that the girl had a favorite pair of shoes that tapped when she ran.

"She called them her 'clackity-clack shoes,' and they were her favorites. We buried her in them," Jennifer's mom said, choking back a sob. (To remind you, Jennifer died after a kidney operation went terribly wrong, leaving her on life support for two days before her parents made the heart-breaking decision to allow her to pass on.)

"The pain and the confusion of that time is gone," I assured her mother. "Right now, I see Jennifer dancing in her favorite yellow dress. In fact, she's prancing around on the Other Side like she owns the place."

"Is . . . is my baby okay? Is she in pain anymore?" Melinda asked. This was truly the reason she'd come to see me—she needed to put her mind at rest because she couldn't get that last sight of her little girl hooked up to all those tubes out of her mind.

"Jennifer is healthy, happy, and free," I said, and Melinda's face took on a luminous quality. I could see where little Jennifer got her spark. "I want you to know that your daughter's okay. Nothing can hurt her anymore."

Melinda mouthed "Thank you" and looked up at the sky.

"Wait, Mom. Now Jennifer is actually acting very bois-terous—she wants me to mention May 9 to you. Does that have any special meaning?" I asked.

At first, I couldn't hear Melinda's reply because Jennifer was giggling so loudly.

"I can't believe it!" Melinda finally proclaimed and then settled back on the couch to tell me a story. It seems that on May 9, a few weeks before her fatal operation, a platter of cupcakes was delivered to the kindergarten class to celebrate Jennifer's birthday.

The teacher hugged Melinda's daughter and told the class, "It's Jennifer's special day, so let's eat our cupcakes and give her our best wishes." (She later called Melinda to tell her that the cupcakes were actually for another Jennifer in a different class!)

When Jennifer came home, she sheepishly told the story to her mom. "It was so silly because Teacher thought it was my birthday today!" she admitted. "I know it was wrong, Mommy, but you know how much I love cupcakes. For me, it did turn into a very special day."

Her mother let her off the hook, and her family deemed May 9 Jennifer's second birthday, or her "very special day." When a smiling Jennifer was tucked into bed that night, her parents had to chuckle at the whole thing. Little did they know that a month later, life would take an unfair turn. . . .

During her 36 hours on life support, Melinda's own mother came to visit her granddaughter. "Soon you'll be able to fly far, far away, but you'll always be our little angel butterfly," she whispered, clutching the little girl's warm hand.

Her family was taking a short break from a vigil at the hospital when Jennifer crossed over. At the exact moment of her passing, her sister, Lisa, stopping running around the yard, looked at a white butterfly in the sky and exclaimed, "See, it's my sister! My sister!"

"Melinda," I said during our reading, "I don't want you to think that you're crazy, because you actually have been seeing Jennifer around the house. She's telling me that she visits you often and is still a vital part of the family."

I could see the stress and pressure leave Melinda's face. It was almost as if I was giving her the okay to believe. "John, the other day I was reading a book in my living room," she said, "and it looked like someone had their face pressed against the glass from the outside. I saw a little girl waving to me. Then I went outside and no one was there," she told me. "Also, everywhere I go, I always see butterflies. For example, the other night, my husband and I took a walk, and this beautiful blue tropical butterfly unlike any I've ever seen in our area settled on the tip of his shoe. It even let my husband transfer it to his hand. It was as if it belonged to us."

I nodded. "Lisa has also seen Jennifer. Right now, Jennifer's saying hello to her sister and brother, too. She wants you to know that she talks to both of them."

"Her little brother says that he keeps hearing sounds. I even thought his ear tubes were blocked, but the doctor said they aren't," Melinda said. "And Lisa was on a field trip the other day when a butterfly landed on her finger and stayed there for a really long time. Everyone thought it was amazing."

Now Jennifer was telling me something so great that I knew I had to share it with her mother. "Your daughter says she loves giving hugs to her brother and sister. And now she can't wait to hug her new baby brother," I told her mother who finally shook her head.

"I'm sorry, John. You're finally wrong here. Jennifer only has one brother," she said.

"Darling, I think what your daughter is telling me is that you're pregnant," I gently said.

Melinda's purse fell to the floor—then she began to laugh and shake her head. "There's absolutely no way that I'm pregnant, but it's a lovely idea," she said.

"Well, let me know what happens," I said. At that moment, Jennifer give me a little wink, and I just knew that another child would soon be entering this family, and that it would be a boy. Of course, Melinda was here to talk about the little girl that she lost, so I let my focus return to her.

"Jennifer wants me to say that she loves her balloons and notes. She says to tell you that she knows you're not planning to do balloons this year, but really wants them, too. Does this mean anything to you?"

Melinda excitedly nodded and said, "Every year since her death, we celebrate Jennifer's birthday by releasing white balloons in the air with messages stuffed inside them saying how much we love her. This year, I ordered butterflies from a local farm that breeds and raises them. I invited each child in Jennifer's class to come to our house and release one butterfly into the sky."

"Well, Mom, your little girl loves that idea, but she says that she also wants her balloons because she looks forward to them."

Melinda's eyes misted over again and she vowed, "There will definitely be balloons this year." Later she told me, "I left your office feeling like a weight had been lifted off my chest. I finally had confirmation that Jennifer was happy and healthy. She was a joyous little girl once again, and I know she's still a big part of our family."

Jennifer is also a very smart cookie. "A week after I came back from Los Angeles, I found out that I was pregnant," Melinda confirmed, and eight months later, a beautiful baby boy joined the family.

After the baby was born, Melinda was standing outside on the front lawn when a long-time friend, who didn't believe any of what Melinda and I had discussed, chose to make a visit. Suddenly, the woman was standing in the center of the lawn in total silence. When Melinda asked what was going on, the woman could only whisper, "I just saw the strangest thing. An image of a little girl who reminds me of Jennifer just ran up behind you and threw her arms around your legs. I saw her do it!"

"This was always Jennifer's way of greeting me in the morning," Melinda reported to me. "Another night, my son saw a ball of light dancing in the front yard. Little Matthew ran in to tell me that he thought it was his sister. I could only smile, because our little angel butterfly was watching over her family. I don't question these sightings anymore, John. Talking to you brought me so much comfort because nobody can ever take my little girl away. Her wings have allowed her to fly high, but she can also come home again."

After such an emotional reading with Melinda, I went to the beach to clear my own head. I was the only one out there, and I sat down in the sand to watch a brilliant sunset. As I stared into the horizon, I couldn't help but notice something slowly washing up on the shore. As I walked toward it, I couldn't believe my eyes. It was a single red balloon. Somehow I feel it was a thank you sent special delivery . . . compliments of Jennifer.

◎

Of course, it's the ultimate tragedy to lose a child, but as you can see from these stories, children are God's resilient little troopers. Parents can go on, knowing that their daughters and sons are safe, whole, beautiful, and free from pain. They're making connections with their families both here and on the Other Side, and they'll continue to do so forever.

—— ◎ ——

chapter 12

OUR PARENTS

OUR PARENTS ARE THE ULTIMATE history teachers because they have our pasts memorized—they even remember every tear we shed as children. Our stories are their stories because they were a part of them from the beginning. Even as adults, our mothers and fathers allow us to be children again in their presence—all of a sudden, we're not CEOs or teachers or nurses anymore—we're just their kids. In the best type of situations, our parents are our anchors, even if we've moved thousands of miles away or see them only at holidays.

The loss of a parent at any age is often one of the saddest facts of life. I don't care if we're 15 or 60 when a parent passes on—the mourning process is always a rough one. We're forced to say good-bye to our first champions.

I've spoken with many people over the years who have lost their parents, but Dick and Sue's stories really stand out to me.

Remember the Music

A handsome East Coast radio announcer with one of the most mellifluous voices I'd ever heard, Dick called after hearing me do a few readings on a late-night talk show.

"On my own radio show, I'd interviewed a few psychics over the years," Dick says today. "It never amounted to much of anything, so I don't know why I bothered listening to you, John. But as I did, I heard the most amazing connections being made for the lucky people who called in."

It turns out that Dick had just lost his beloved father a few months before hearing the show, and his grief was agonizing. In many ways, Dick felt a bit confused about it because losing a parent was a fact of life when one reached his age. "I'm certainly not a little boy anymore, but what can I tell you? My father was one of my best friends in the world," Dick says now. "When I got the news that my Dad had died, without even giving me a chance to tell him how I felt or how much I loved him, I was devastated. I felt like a small child who had lost the most precious person to him."

Dick's father was a healthy 69-year-old man who had just gone in for a physical where the docs proclaimed that he was perfectly healthy. To celebrate, he hopped on a plane and went to visit his sister in Florida. At her house, he indulged in one of his favorite rituals.

"Dad got in a hot bath to read the evening paper, which to him was the height of luxury," Dick explains. But after quite a bit of time had passed, Dick's aunt became concerned and burst into the bathroom to find that her beloved brother had had a heart attack and passed away in the tub. "It was just an instantaneous heart attack. He probably didn't even know what happened, which is one of the kindest ways to pass," Dick says.

Dick contacted me, and months later, we had a phone reading. He was open-minded, but didn't expect much to happen. He knew that I didn't know anything about him or his dad, so he was rather surprised when the first thing out of my mouth was, "So, you want to know about your dad. He's here, and he wants to communicate with you, too."

I didn't know what Dick's father's name was yet, so I asked him about the name I kept hearing: "Carl." It was a simple inquiry, and I couldn't imagine why Dick was suddenly silent on the other end of the phone.

He finally explained that his father was called Max his entire life, but his real name was Carl, a fact that Dick didn't even know until an aunt had told him at his father's funeral. "I thought that Carl was just some middle name he dropped, but it was his given first name," Dick said.

I told him that his father always hated the name Carl, which is why he changed it to Max at an early age. (Dick would later ask his aunt and find out that was true.) A moment later, I discovered that Max was a huge fan of music.

"Dick, why am I hearing something that sounds like *Jolie?*" I asked him. "Your dad keeps saying 'Jolie, Jolie, Jolie.'" Suddenly, I started hearing music in my ears, jazz at its finest. I passed that on to Dick as well.

I could hear him quietly sobbing. Moments later, with a shaking voice, he told me that ever since he was a teenager, he and his father loved to listen to Al Jolson—whose nickname was Jolie—on his pop's old phonograph.

"Dad wants me to remind you to keep listening to Jolie and think of him when you do. He's listening where he is now," I said, and Dick began to cry louder.

"I needed an entire box of Kleenex," he said later. "My father and I shared Al Jolson for 25 years—for us, it was like other guys and their fathers playing baseball. So his saying to 'remember Jolie' was better than hearing 'I love you.' "

That wasn't the end of the surprises in store for Dick during our reading. Next I received some information from his father that I knew might prove to be a bit controversial. Again, when I hear a message from spirit, I have to pass it on even if there will be consequences, so I plowed ahead. "Dick, your father's telling me that there's someone else he's sending his love to besides you, his daughters, and his sisters. He wants you to know that he had a girlfriend."

Dick began to laugh. "Now, John, I have to disagree with you. In fact, you're totally wrong here. Even though my parents divorced years ago, Dad never had any romantic relationships—and I'd know because I talked to him every single day."

"Please keep an open mind here for a minute," I told him. "Your father says that his girlfriend of several years lived on the floor above his in the apartment building, and he had very strong feelings for her. He wants her to know that he's sending her his love—perhaps you could pass on the message to her." Dick still couldn't believe it, but he said that he'd check into it later on.

Finally, I had one last message for Dick: "Your father wants you to call your sister." When he said that he talked to his sister all the time, I replied, "She's having neck and back problems. Dad really wants you to help her, Dick. He's worried because she's in a lot of pain."

After our reading, Dick was concerned and immediately called his sister Ellen, who swore that she wasn't in any sort of pain. "But you know what?" Ellen said. "It's our *other* sister who's really hurting."

It turns out that Dick had been on the outs with his second sister for some time, and his father was staging his own unexpected "family reunion." And so, only due to his father's wishes, Dick placed a call to the sister with whom he hadn't spoken for some time.

"Oh, Dick, I'm so glad you called me! I miss you, and I'm having such a hard time with this agonizing back and neck trouble," she said.

Instantly, the family was reunited—and Dick offered to help her in any way possible. He also shared a few of the messages from their father, while, in turn, his sister had some news for him. "Dad *did* have a wonderful girlfriend who lived in the building with him, but he kept it to himself because he wasn't sure how we kids would handle it," she said.

Today Dick marvels, "A few years later, I lost my mother, who was also another wonderful friend in my life. Honestly, I ache for Mom and Dad every day, but being able to sit at a table for an hour and connect with their souls puts me at ease. During that hour, I always feel like the luckiest man in the world because I have my best friends 'on the line' with me— although it's a serious long-distance connection."

The Story of Snowball

I can't help but smile when people make a checklist before they come to see me. These people always expect to hear what they *want* to hear, but as usual, they get what they *need* to hear. This especially surprised a hardworking and thoroughly charming single mother from Boston named Sue, whose friends told her about me and urged her to make an appointment.

At the time of our meeting, I was doing my psychic and medium consultations in my apartment in Cambridge. Today my main focus is on my mediumship, but when Sue knocked on my door on that cool November evening, she was only interested in my psychic abilities. She was dating two guys and wanted to know who was the better romantic partner, as if I were hosting the "Psychic Dating Game." As she says today, "I hate to admit it, but I wanted John to tell me about my love life and my future at work—period!"

As soon as I met her, I knew that Sue had some education ahead of her. "Sue, do you have some sort of exam coming up? I'm not sure if you're in school, but I see you taking a written test. Somehow this test has to do with your job. The results are good, and if you apply yourself, you'll become very successful at work."

Sue smiled because this was *exactly* what she'd been looking for. Although she was a busy mom who didn't have much free time, she'd managed to squeeze in classes that would help her advance at her job.

"I see you obtaining some sort of paper that will allow you to do what you really want to do," I told her.

"I need a certificate so that I can work on bigger projects at work," she said.

"Wait a minute, now I'm getting confused here. Why am I hearing the name Jeff twice? Are there two Jeffs in your life?"

"Yes, I'm dating 'the two Jeffs,'" she said, her voice brimming with excitement.

"Sue, I don't see either of them around in the long term," I told her, knowing that wasn't what she wanted to hear, but I always have to be honest. "I see them as definite ex-boyfriends. Neither are very good at relationships at this time, but I think you've seen those signs already."

Sue nodded because she knew it was true. Sometimes it just takes an outside observer to state the obvious.

"I see another man in your life who's there for the long term," I continued, "but it's much deeper than a romantic relationship. Do you have . . . a son?"

"Yes, I have a wonderful son," said Sue. "He's the best kid in the whole wide—"

I hated to interrupt her, but a spirit was trying to link with me was so strongly that she insisted that her presence be made known. "I'm sorry, Sue, but your mom has passed, correct? This is a bit strange, but she keeps calling your son, 'My boy, my boy.'"

At that point, Sue's mouth dropped open in astonishment because she knew exactly what I was talking about. "I'm not sure I understand this part, but she thanks you for bringing 'my boy' to see her,'" I said.

"It's Mom," said Sue, crying now. "John, my mother passed two years ago, and she always called *my* son 'my boy.' The three of us lived together for years—my son and I lived upstairs, while Mom was downstairs. Then I got this new job, and we moved a few hundred miles away from her. But I tried to bring my son to visit her as much as possible."

"She knew you had to get on with your life, and she thanks you for all those hours spent in the car driving him to see her," I said. "She knows you tried to bring him by the night before she died."

Through her tears, Sue said, "Mom was very sick, and I told her that I'd bring her grandson to see her, but she said, 'No, honey. I'm tired and I'll see him later. Tell him I love him, and I love you, too.' She passed the next day."

I gave her a moment to compose herself, and then I told her that her mom didn't want her to feel guilty. Sue admitted that she had indeed been carrying some heavy feelings around about moving away and leaving her mother all alone.

"Your mom says that now she gets to see her boy whenever she wants to," I said. "She also wants you to know that she's not alone. In fact, she's here with . . . someone you weren't really fond of—she's scratching his head right now."

"Oh, no!" Sue said, laughing now. "I can't believe that my mother found her tabby cat, the one that made me sneeze. Frankly, I could never stand him because of his mean disposition, but my mom loved him so much."

In my head, I kept hearing Sue's mother tell me, "Say Snowball, say Snowball." I couldn't figure out if that was the cat's name, or did Sue like to ski? From my training, I knew I had to trust and always give what I got, so I proceeded. "Sue, why is your mom saying, 'Snowball, Snowball'?"

At that point, Sue's smile softened. "She's really saying, 'Snowball'?" she asked in an amazed voice. "Snowball is my son, John, and you'll have to pardon me a minute because I think I'm going to have a heart attack right now. *How could you possibly have known that?* No one except my immediate family knows that my mom used to call my son by this nickname."

"Please, Sue," I said with a grin, "no heart attacks during my sessions." Pausing for a moment, I finally answered her question by stating, "Sue, I didn't know anything until your mom told me."

At that point, Sue told me the entire story. "My son is 20 now, but the day he chose to be born was dramatic. It was during one of the biggest blizzards ever to hit the East Coast, but it was in April, so no one was prepared for it. Immediately after having the baby, I called my family and begged them not to come to the hospital because driving would be insane—there were 20 inches of snow with high winds and drifting walls of ice." One person, however, couldn't be stopped—and that was Sue's mother.

"On a night when even the snowplow operators had quit because they couldn't drive anymore, my mother got into her little car and spent six hours driving the few miles to the hospital to see her baby grandson. I couldn't believe it when the door to my hospital room burst open, and my mom pushed all the nurses away with snow falling off of her. 'Okay, where is he?' she demanded. I handed her the baby, and the first thing she did was toss off her snow-covered parka and say, 'Oh, you're Grandma's little Snowball.' From that day on, she called my son either Snowball or Snow."

"Sue, your mom says she knows that her little Snowball is fine and happy. He's doing well, which makes her proud. She sends her love to both of you, and most of all, she wants you to stop worrying, because she isn't alone. In fact, she says she's sitting here with another family friend—he doesn't talk, but he's wonderful company. He's licking her hand right now." I stopped for a second. "Did your mom have a beagle?"

"Yes, and if you're telling me that he's sitting—"

"On her feet," I said.

"Yes, that's where he always sat," said Sue, who laughed again and said, "Now, I think I'm really going to need an ambulance."

I smiled. "Sue, your mom wants you to go home and give her boy a hug and whisper in his ear that Grandma will always be watching over her Snowball."

Sue was beaming as she got up from her chair, gave me a hug, and shook her head. She'd come to me to get information about her love life, but she walked away knowing that her mother was always in her heart.

As I walked her out, we both noticed the first signs of winter. A single, perfect snowflake fell gently between us.

There are no easy ways to push past the grief of losing a loved one, especially a parent who will always be one of your biggest influences. Many people get help by talking about their grief with others or by joining a support group. I also want to stress that there's no time limit on when your grief should end. Shock, denial, and sadness can last a very long time, and you can't flip a switch to turn it off. Go at your own pace, and remember that your parents are still with you in spirit and they're always your rocks. You can lean on them even when you don't think they're there—because really . . . they never left.

chapter 13

PARTNERS FOREVER

WHEN YOU'RE STANDING AT THE altar pledging true love, the words "till death do us part" seem like a romantic, storybook promise without real consequences. Beautiful brides and their handsome grooms make this vow thinking that they really *will* grow old together—few ever think about what it would mean to lose a partner forever.

How you deal with this type of loss depends, naturally, on the circumstances. If the death is sudden, then there's the horrible feeling of not being able to say good-bye to your soul mate. In a long-term illness situation, you hopefully do get a chance to express what's in your heart, but you might also have to watch your loved one suffer. There's also the feelings of guilt coupled with relief that your mate has finally passed and isn't in pain anymore. Please know that these types of emotions are normal—*no one* wants to see anyone they care for suffer.

In either type of loss, there are unanswered questions: *Did I say enough? Did I do enough?* There's often anger at the universe or a loss of faith in a Higher Power. Again, these are natural responses to grief, and it doesn't matter how old you are or how long you've been with your partner.

The following stories remain two of my favorite examples of how true love never dies.

Island Girl

Tad was struggling with a broken heart when he flew all the way from the tropical islands of Turks and Caicos to see me. To be honest, I was a bit nervous about his visit because he was investing so much in meeting with me—including an expensive plane ticket; a hotel stay; and a long, exhausting flight.

"I can't promise I'll make a connection or guarantee who will come through," I warned him when he called to make the appointment.

He sounded sad, yet hopeful, as he replied, "I know that, John, but I just need to take this chance."

Tad arrived on a sunny morning, and after pouring him some coffee for his jet lag, we sat down. Immediately, I began to make contact with his father and brother who had passed on. But deep down, I felt they were here just to bring someone else through to Tad. "They want me to tell you that they're taking care of the most important person in the world to you," I said. Tad's father gave me some more information, and I asked Tad, "Do you understand the name Tracy?"

Tad began to nod his head and said, "My wife's name is Tracy. Oh my God, I just knew that I was right when I decided to make this trip!"

Tad and Tracy's love story wasn't your typical one, but it was one of the most touching I've ever heard in my life. Tracy had cancer for many years, and Tad fell in love with her and married her when she was in the middle of chemotherapy. Their love transcended the weaknesses of the human body, and he was glued to her side during all the years of treatment that would make up the end of her life. Then again, it wasn't hard to love Tracy, who, even when she was in pain, devoted herself to helping the children on the islands lead better lives.

"First of all, Tracy says that she's still with you, and she'll continue to be by your side forever. She loves you so very much, Tad," I said. "She's thanking you for the memorial. Wait—she's telling me that there were *two* memorials. And where's this beautiful garden that she's showing me?"

Tad acknowledged that he planted a memorial garden to celebrate his wife's life, and even ordered a nice plaque with her name engraved on it to put near the flowers. But the company who sent it didn't include the specially sized mounting screws for the stake that Tad needed to secure the plaque into the ground—so he simply propped it up in his wife's garden against a few rocks. The company subsequently sent another plaque with the correct materials, so Tad put that in the garden, too. There were Tracy's two memorials.

"Where's this babbling brook that I keep hearing in the background?" I asked.

Tad dissolved into tears. Finally, he was able to explain that there were no rivers or streams where he lived, and his beloved Tracy found the sound of running water to be very calming. So Tad had taken great pains to create an entire water system to run through the roses and tulips in Tracy's garden.

I continued. "Your wife wants you to know that soon there will be some dramatic changes in your life. You might not see this now, but it will soon become apparent. She knows what you're thinking—this has nothing to do with your joining her. She wants you to know that she's waiting for you, but you shouldn't be in any hurry to be with her. You still have a lot of work to do here."

I could only smile as I told Tad a few particulars about his wife. "She had a genuine love of people, especially children. In fact, she worked with them, didn't she?" I said.

Tad nodded. "She was a wonderful junior high school teacher."

As our session came to an end, I told Tad that Tracy might be sending him a sign from time to time to remind him that she was still with him. That very night, he returned to his hotel room, and on his pillow was a small note saying that the person who had turned down his bed that evening and put that chocolate on his pillow was named . . . Tracy.

Today, Tad says, "Needless to say, I still can't see through my tears when I think about the information you gave me that day, John. I'm still waiting for the dramatic changes—not with fear, but with anticipation. I thank you from the bottom of my heart."

Remember the Swans

I immediately liked Ruth, an attractive, soft-spoken woman in her 60s who worked as a real estate agent in Florida. She had beautiful cornflower-blue eyes and a warm smile, but I could see that she was clearly in pain.

"I just wanted to see if there was something to this medium work," she said. "I need some answers, and I'm not sure where else to turn. So my favorite cousin suggested you as a possible solution."

But before I could start my session, she had a little confession to make. "John, I'm not what you'd call a total believer," she said, looking down at her toes as if such a statement might offend me.

I just smiled at her and said, "Ruth, many people come to see me, and just about all of them are thinking the same thing. *Everyone* should be a little skeptical. I admire the fact that you were brave enough to say it." I touched her hand and gently said, "Let's just see what happens."

Ruth's self-confidence seemed to spike a bit when she saw that I wasn't judging her belief system . . . and soon some very special messages would turn those beliefs around.

"Ruth, I feel like I have a husband figure here. Do you have a husband who's crossed?"

"Why, yes!" she said. "My Eddie!"

"Ruth, I know a lot of men don't like to wear rings, but I feel like Eddie liked to wear two. In fact, he's showing me two rings on one hand. Is that right?"

Ruth began to weep and smile at the same time. She told me that Eddie had passed away six months before, and he was buried with his favorite two rings. "He wore his own late father's wedding ring on one finger, and our wedding ring on another," she said.

My hand went up to my chest as I said, "What's with his heart?"

Ruth told me that Eddie had passed from a massive heart attack.

"There's a lot of love coming through here, Ruth. This is a man who doted on you. He had a strong personality. Correct?"

Ruth nodded.

"He's sending you his strength because you keep thinking he's far away. And now he keeps showing me pages and pages of lists. Do you understand this?"

"He always made lists to get everything accomplished. Everyone loved him because he was always in control and got the job done," Ruth said.

"I see him in a uniform."

"Eddie was an officer in the Navy during World War II. Later on, he took that strong personality and became a very successful businessman," she said with a smile. "He was at the top of his field, which was mechanical engineering. He even owned his own company."

"He's talking about how he almost passed twice, but he fooled the doctors," I said. "He knows you were there for him, and he thanks you so much for helping him when he was sick. He's in total good health now and not attached to his old, failing body anymore. He's telling me there were multiple things wrong with him, but why am I being drawn to my back?"

"He had a kidney transplant," Ruth said.

"He was a trouper—they had to drag him into the spirit world." I touched my heart again. "What's with the feeling in my chest? I'm seeing stitches there. Did they operate on his heart as well?"

"Yes, he also had a heart transplant," Ruth said, hugging herself.

"Your love gave him a lot of the strength that kept him here during many amazing struggles. In fact, his love for you willed him to stay on this earth much longer." At this point, I was getting emotional, which I shouldn't do—but this was such an amazing story. I cleared my throat and continued. "Ruth, why does he keep saying to me over and over that he wants you to . . . remember the swans? What does that mean?"

Ruth suddenly turned white. She forced herself to take a few deep breaths before she could find the composure to speak.

"What is that, Ruth? What does it mean?" I gently prodded her.

Finally, she managed to explain. "We used to sit on our favorite bench on our property and look at these magnificent white swans that lived on the lake. One afternoon, Eddie turned to me and said, 'Ruth, you see those swans out there? Swans mate forever—just like us, Ruthie. We're a pair of old swans.'"

I could see Ruth reliving this happy memory. At that moment, it was as if she were back with Eddie on their bench at dusk, holding hands and looking out on a scene that would make an artist want to pick up a paintbrush.

When I felt that Ruth was ready to continue, I said, "Now Eddie's wondering, 'Why aren't you out with your friends? Just because I'm not there doesn't mean you have to stay in the house.'"

"I have a hard time going out because he's not with me," she agreed.

"But he *is* with you, Ruth," I said. "Eddie wants you to continue to have those dinner parties. He wants you to remember the fun times together, but also surround yourself with your friends so that you can have good times in the future." I paused for a moment. "I see roses—I usually don't give flowers in a sitting because they're so common. Everybody gets flowers, but Eddie's handing you *a lot* of roses."

Ruth smiled. "He did love to give me flowers. On my 60th birthday, he took me to our favorite restaurant. Before a special cake was delivered for dessert, Eddie had the waiter bring over the 60 long-stemmed roses he'd purchased for the occasion."

"Well, he's adding a few more to the bunch," I said. "I hope this helps you believe—not just for today, but forever."

"John, I'll try to find it in me to be with my friends

because I do miss them terribly. It will be easier now that I know Eddie's with me." With that, she smiled, thinking that her session was over.

But I had one more thing to tell her. "Ruth, do you understand this? Now Eddie's talking about you gazing out the window every morning into your garden. Is there something else there besides flowers?"

Ruth was beaming now. "Before Eddie got sick, he bought me two beautiful ceramic swans to put in my garden," she said. "I still have those swans, even though they're very old and weathered now. Still, every morning I look at them the first moment I open my eyes. And yes, I will remember the swans. Forever."

To cope with the loss of your life partner, the best advice I can give you is that they wouldn't want you to suffer alone, in silence. I recommend that you talk to someone about your feelings, be it a close friend or a professional therapist. It also doesn't help when you close yourself off from those who were around you when you were part of a couple. Sometimes the spouse who's left on Earth feels as if they're not welcome in the old group, or they feel guilty about socializing. It does take some guts to go out alone and blend back into the group. Often, you might find that your friends avoid the subject of your loss because they don't want to upset you. Yet true healing comes from talking about how you miss your beloved partner. Healing can only occur when you deal with your confusion, anger, and grief and know that you can stand on your own . . . with your loved one standing right beside you.

chapter 14

TRAGIC LOSSES

EACH TIME SOMEONE CROSSES over to the Other Side, there are, of course, many who mourn the loss. When a loved one leaves after living a *long* life, there can be some acceptance that this is the natural flow of the universe. However, when someone is taken in a tragic and sudden way, it often leaves their friends or family wondering, *How could this happen?*

The worst part for survivors is imagining what it was like for their loved one during his or her last moments. Grief counselors agree that this is the most detrimental thing that people can do, because the imagination has a way of turning what actually happened into something far worse. People can even drive themselves to the brink of madness thinking about all the possibilities. My advice is to take out photo albums of loved ones and try to picture them prior to their death, rather than trying to sort out what happened when they passed on

Of course, the entire country is still dealing with grief over the tragedy of September 11, 2001, and we're still in mourning for the loss of our security and innocence. There's something very unusual about this type of shared grief, because just looking at your neighbors' shocked and sad faces confirms that this is *real,* and there's no turning back from the emotional work that needs to be done to sort out your feelings.

Sharing your sadness is an excellent way of recovering from a tragic loss. And if you know someone who's suffering from this sort of turmoil, really the only thing you can say to them is: "I'm here for you, in whatever way you need me. I want you to know that I'm feeling sad, too, and I'm more than willing to share my sadness with you and be a witness to your grief."

I was the middleman when it came to two very different tragic losses—one concerning a child, and the other focusing on a slain police officer. Each of these accounts illustrates how a spirit can soar above even the most difficult of struggles.

The Locket

There are times when life deals us such a severe blow that it doesn't seem like healing is even going to be a possibility. That was the case with Donna, a mother of five from New Jersey. A few years ago, she was sitting in her home with her two sets of identical twins . . . and an empty chair. On that spring evening, the family was trying to push away the family tragedy that had occurred and engage in some mindless fun. Relaxing in their den, Donna and the children were flipping through the channels and fighting over what to watch when they settled upon *Unsolved Mysteries.* It happened to be the episode that featured my story. Immediately afterwards, Donna jumped up and e-mailed me for an appointment.

Donna had spoken to other psychics since the death of her 16-year-old daughter, Michelle, but she'd received little satisfaction, because none of the psychics or mediums she'd contacted had any concrete evidence that might turn her into a believer. "When I found your number, I didn't think I'd invest time in traveling from my home in Jersey to your office in New Hampshire because, honestly, I didn't really believe a medium could reach my little girl," she says today. "That's why I only asked you for a phone reading."

Settled in our respective homes, we began the session. As usual, the only thing I knew about Donna was that she was a female from New Jersey. The rest would have to come from the spirit world.

"Donna, there's somebody on the Other Side—someone female, who's saying that you miss her. Could it be a sister? Hang on. This is someone much younger. Wait, did you lose a daughter?"

"Yes, I did," Donna said in a voice so weary from pain that I could barely hear her.

In an instant, I knew that she hadn't lost her daughter due to an illness or a car accident. This was the worst possible scenario of all, and I felt a ringing in my brain. "She was murdered, wasn't she?" I asked. "Someone hurt her head and violated her in other ways."

At that moment, I noticed something strange in the usually peaceful and tranquil office of my home. The lights were wildly flickering on and off, as if I was getting my confirmation before Donna could even answer.

"Yes, my daughter was killed violently," she whispered.

The minute Donna said the words, I couldn't help but notice that her daughter was also giving me her own affirmation of events. "Are your lights doing anything?" I asked Donna.

"No, nothing yet," she said.

"Mine are flickering like crazy now," I told her, moving along because I didn't want her to be disappointed that the same thing wasn't going on in her home. "Is there some significance to July 4th?"

"My Michelle died 13 years ago on July 4th," Donna said, her voice cracking.

At that point, I had to tell her something that I hoped would provide some relief: "Donna, your daughter is telling me that she's standing next to you right now, and you're wearing her ring."

Donna could only gasp. "I've been wearing the ring ever since the day she died."

"But you don't wear it on your ring finger."

"No, I wear it on my pinkie," Donna said. "Michelle always wore it on her pinkie, too."

Slowly, Donna recounted a story that was so horrific that I needed to gather myself together when she finished. Thirteen years ago, Michelle received a call from some family friends in Florida who had three young sons and needed a summer baby-sitter. They asked if Michelle was interested. It would require her to move out of state for three months and live full time with the family

Donna's next words were laced with guilt. "I didn't want to send her and told them no, but these friends begged me because they needed the help." Michelle thought that it might be a great adventure to move away and be on her own. "We made a deal that if she worked hard in school, she could take the job," Donna said.

A week after Michelle arrived in Florida, she was playing with her young charges on the beach when she began talking to a friendly young couple who eventually invited her to a July 4th bash. Knowing that she didn't have her own car, they offered to pick her up and drive her home later. The teen was in a quandary and immediately made a long-distance call to her mother.

"She wanted to see if it would be okay," Donna recalls. "I told her to make sure to give me the couple's names, their address, and their driver's license numbers. I couldn't think how I could be a better parent then to ask for all this information."

It turns out that Michelle did go to the party, but the couple was very busy and couldn't drive her home when she wanted to leave. Michelle offered to walk the few miles back, and one of the other partygoers, a lean man in his 20s, insisted, "Let me walk you so you'll be safe."

On the way home, he raped her and hit her in the head. The end result was that Michelle died instantly, and Donna received that horrifying middle-of-the-night phone call that every parent dreads. Later, she would learn that this man had a history of attacking young girls in several different states.

Donna was told that the two consecutive 25-year sentences in the state penitentiary he received for Michelle's murder should ease her mind. But, as she told me in a defiant voice, "*Nothing* eases your mind when your child is suddenly taken away in such a violent manner."

"Did Michelle talk to you a lot about death and the afterlife right before her passing?" I asked her.

"Yes—how did you know?" Donna was flabbergasted. She went on to give me a few more details. "I had a near-death experience during my last pregnancy. I never talked about it with my children because I thought it might frighten them. But the day before Michelle left for Florida, she begged me to tell her what I'd experienced when I almost died. Then she said that if *she* died, she wanted to be buried with certain things. It was as if she had a weird premonition."

"The spirit often knows when it's about to move on," I told her. Next I asked, "What's with the butterflies?"

"Just before her death, Michelle read a book about how children in concentration camps during the Holocaust used to draw butterflies on the walls, which was a symbol to them of freedom and life after death. The day we buried Michelle, I walked to my sister's front door after the services, and an unbelievable amount of yellow butterflies instantly surrounded me. It was very strange and moving."

"Michelle has contacted you in other ways, too, hasn't she?" I asked Donna. "Why do I smell Ivory soap?"

For the first time, Donna actually laughed, because the memory brought her more pleasure than heartache. "Michelle was the only one in our house who liked Ivory soap," she explained, "and since her death, I've never purchased one bar of the stuff. But every once in a while, an entire room will fill up with the smell of it, and then, just as suddenly, slowly disappear."

"Michelle loves the fact that you still bake her a birthday cake," I told her.

"Every single year, I bake her a cake to celebrate her life," Donna confirmed.

"She also loves the angels," I said.

Donna didn't speak for a moment, but when she composed herself, she told me that after Michelle's death, the family took two wooden angels and placed them on both sides of her headstone. "The message is that she's still part of our lives, except now she's our angel," she said.

"Donna, what's with the locket?" I asked. "Did your daughter have a necklace that perhaps you've tucked away as a special memory?"

She paused. "No one in my house has a locket," she said, sounding a bit worried as if she was letting me down.

"Well, keep that in the back of your mind, because there might be something with a locket and Michelle that will happen in the future."

Our conversation proved to Donna that her daughter was still with her, in no pain and free of the turmoil of her death. Later, I found out that Michelle had a few other gifts in store for her mother. Almost a year after our reading, Donna took out the tape she'd made of our phone conversation, poured a cup of coffee, and pushed "play" on her tape recorder. Immediately, the lights in her kitchen began to flicker wildly. As she told me later, "The strange thing is that the clocks on my microwave clock and coffee maker didn't lose a minute. I didn't have to reset them like I do when there's a storm."

Each time Donna pushed the "play" button on her tape recorder, the lights did their little dance. "I knew it was my angel, and I could feel her sitting in her chair at the kitchen table," she said.

Soon afterwards, Donna was cleaning out her sweater drawer, and a tiny box that was wedged way in the back caught her eye. It didn't look familiar, so she carefully opened it. Inside wasn't a ring or a bracelet . . . it was a beautiful heart locket. It turns out that one of Donna's other daughters had purchased the keepsake after her sister died and placed the most beautiful photo of Michelle inside of it. But since her mother was so upset at the funeral, the young girl didn't want to add to her mother's grief by giving Donna something that would surely add to her pain. So she tucked it away in the drawer for a rainy day and then forgot about it.

Slowly, Donna opened the little silver heart and saw Michelle's stunning face staring back at her. Her heart filled with love and joy knowing that Michelle was right there beside her. Then her eyes gravitated toward an open window; when she walked closer to it, the breeze softly caressed her face. Donna closed her eyes, and when she opened them, she noticed that on the windowsill was the most beautiful yellow butterfly she'd ever seen.

Michelle's mom received two special gifts that morning that she'll treasure forever.

The Sarge

One night during an intermission at one of my lectures, I took a quick walk outside the lecture hall to prepare myself for the next part of the evening. It was my way of revving myself up for the demonstration, which, frankly, was why everyone was there that evening. I wanted to make it a special night, and all the signs were a "go." I'd already started to link, and was in the process of sorting out who wanted to come through first—or more to the point, which spirit had the loudest voice.

As I was walking back down the corridor, still clearing space in my mind, a gentleman walked up to me, catching me off-guard. He introduced himself as Joe and thanked me for the work that I did. He told me that it was very important for him to be there that evening because he'd just left the hospital, where in the last few hours his dying mother had been given her last rites. When the hospital staff told him that he should take a break, he knew exactly where he should go. He told me that he felt as though he *had* to attend this event, which he had tickets for.

I found out that Joe was quite open-minded and knowledgeable when it came to psychic matters. He certainly wasn't one of the more typical men in the audience, who were usually dragged to these lectures by their wives. Joe seemed to be the leader in his family group that night, and told me that several of his relatives were in the hall.

I told him that I wished the very best for his family and especially his ailing mother. Sometimes good wishes are just Band-Aids, and I could see from the pain in his eyes that he and I both knew that his mother would be leaving this world very soon. We shook hands, and he opened the door for me as both of us walked back inside.

It was time to start the demonstration, and the audience of 200 was busily settling down after the break. I spotted Joe sitting about ten rows back, and because I didn't think he'd mind, I quietly approached him and asked if I could tell the audience what he'd just told me about his mother. He said okay. I related his story to the audience, but more important, I shared how Joe's strength and his belief in the spirit world was helping him and his family at this difficult time. I asked everyone to take a few moments to say a prayer for his mom and his family, hoping that we could send them a lot of love and strength.

Immediately afterwards, I felt a presence draw near. I acknowledged the spirit with a few words, and even though it was quite the coincidence, I knew the message was for Joe. Everything else would have to wait for a few minutes longer—Joe needed to hear this.

"Joe, I have someone with me who has just jumped to the front of the line. Do you want to pick up the phone and talk?"

"Sure, John, go ahead," he said. He was totally calm, contained, and clearly in control of his emotions. He didn't appear remotely phased by my directness either—it was as if he was ready and waiting.

"Who's the cop?" I asked.

"We lost a very close and dear friend who was a state trooper," Joe replied without any hesitation.

"Well, this must be him, because I feel as though I should call him 'sir.'" I started to reach up to my shoulder and felt a few stripes of his uniform. "He must have had a rank, because I can feel the stripes of his uniform. Do you understand this?"

"Oh, yes! He was a sergeant."

"I'm hearing the name Jimmy or James," I continued, as the link grew stronger and the evidence kept on being fed my way.

"That's Jim!"

"He's telling me that his passing was fast and totally unexpected. He says that he died outside with a large group of people around."

I noticed that Joe's family was whispering to each other in excitement. I could feel this officer's strength as well as his kindness and love for his relatives and friends. This guy was a true hero type, someone whom everybody loved, and who would risk his own life to help out a stranger.

Joe said, "Yes, he died in the line of duty. He was shot and killed outside, in front of a crowd of bystanders who had gathered at the scene. We miss him so much, and his passing was tragic for everyone involved."

Joe later told me that Jim had been on duty when he was summoned to a domestic disturbance call. A man had barricaded himself inside a house and was waving around a shotgun. Soon, the suspect was at the window and wildly shooting at the police officers stationed outside. Although Jim was wearing his regulation Kevlar vest, a bullet hit him at an odd angle, sneaking under his arm and penetrating his heart. He died instantly.

"Why is he showing me the number 502?" I asked, sensing the level of emotion steadily rising, both in Joe's group and around the hall.

"That was his cruiser number," Joe said, as his entire family looked at each other in shock.

"Hey, Joe, the Sarge is a strong communicator. He was strong here in this life, and he's just as strong over there. He's sending his love to his wife and children and to the rest of his family. He wants to thank them for the memorial. Oh, wait a minute, he just corrected me. There were *two* memorials. He's very particular and wants me to know about both of them."

"Absolutely," said Joe. "One was on the anniversary of his death, and the other is a scholarship fund we set up in his name."

There was a ripple of gasps around the audience.

"He loves that!" I said. "Now he keeps showing me the letters *D.D.*" It was as though the letters were being written above my head, yet only I could see them.

"That's my brother, Dennis. Those are his initials," Joe said, his voice quivering ever-so-slightly. "He just goes by D.D. Jim and Dennis were great friends."

"Tell D.D. that the Sarge says hello," I continued with a salute.

"We will, we will."

By now, the mood in the hall was electrifying. All eyes were fixed on either Joe or me. It was so still that you could hear each of the old wooden chairs moan under the pressure of the people sitting in them. Knowing that people were captivated, I went on. "Jim's calling out to his 'baby'—a daughter, I believe."

"Yes, he called his youngest daughter 'the baby.'"

I can always tell when I'm talking to an Irish person because I'll see shamrocks or feel something about St. Patrick's Day in my mind. "Jim must be Irish, because he's showing me shamrocks and a statue of St. Patrick."

"You got that right, John!" Joe chuckled. "Jim was Irish through and through."

"Now I'm picking up someone else who's butting in on the line, but he's standing near Jim. Bill wants to say hello. Do you know him?" I asked.

"Oh my God, yes! Our friend Bill passed away a year ago in a snowmobile accident." I noticed now that Joe and his family were all holding hands.

"Well, he's hanging out with Jim now." I could feel the two men on the Other Side, and they were standing side-by-side, smiling proudly, and obviously pleased to be joining me onstage.

An image of Jim's tombstone and a photo of him that appeared to be floating in front of the stone was being given to me. I knew there was a strong connection somehow. "Wow! Joe, he's showing me his tombstone, and somehow his photo is associated with it."

Joe was nodding his head as I presented this important piece of evidence. "His photo and his cruiser are beautifully etched on the tombstone!" he said.

"He's so close to both his family and yours, Joe. He keeps asking me to tell them that he loves them all and that he's fine."

Then came the extraordinary message, one I knew I had to deliver with the utmost sensitivity. "Joe, Jim wants me to tell you that he'll be there for your mother when she arrives. He's also telling me that she almost passed a few times but kept fooling the doctors. He's waiting to greet her and take her on her final journey."

"That's correct. We did almost lose her a few times."

"I'm sorry, Joe, it's getting crowded up here. Someone else is jumping in now. Who's Margaret?" I nodded to my left, acknowledging the spirit who had come so close.

Joe's wife, Karen, raised her hand, introducing herself. She said her mom was Margaret, and that she was still living.

"Did she have a sister who passed, who probably had dementia or Alzheimer's disease?"

All Karen could do was nod her head as her family looked in her direction.

"She's come through, and says a big hello to Margaret."

"I will. Thank you so much," Karen said quietly.

"Oh, one more thing. She says she's with the construction worker. Do you understand this, Karen?"

Karen confirmed that her dad was, in fact, a construction worker. I was in the process of explaining to the audience that this whole connection came compliments of Jim the state trooper when there was a final tug. It was as though I heard several voices in tandem saying, "Congratulations on the baby!" and I vocalized this.

"Our niece just had a baby!" Karen announced.

"Take Jim's love and know you'll always have an angel of protection watching over you," I told Joe and his family. Just as I started to pull away, the Sarge stepped back once again because this was not a 10-4 for him. I felt as though he really wanted to help one more person get through. "Joe, the Sarge is a persistent guy. He's telling me about the fireman. Who's that?"

Joe was so excited that he almost shouted back his response. "That's me, John! I'm a fireman."

As before, I could feel the intensity all around the room, and the evidence was extraordinary. "Well, somehow I'm connecting with what you do and to the September 11th tragedy at the Twin Towers. You didn't go there, did you, Joe?"

"No, I really wanted to help the people, but my mother needed me," he replied, suddenly looking quite somber.

"Do you or your family know of someone who lost a friend in the Twin Towers?"

Joe's sister-in-law, Connie, who was sitting at the end of the row, raised her hand and explained that she was the one with the September 11 connection. "John, I recently heard from a dear friend of mine that another friend, whom we'd lost touch with, actually lost her husband on the plane that crashed into one of the Towers."

I wasn't sure of the connection to this link, so I asked for more information from the spirit who was trying so hard get a message across. Immediately I heard a *J* name. "Connie, where's the *J* for this man?"

"Connie looked even more surprised. "That's my friend Jane!"

Now the information was coming fast. "So she'd understand the name Robert, correct?" I said.

"Yes, yes, her husband's name is Bob. He's the one who died on the plane."

"Connie, I know that you haven't seen this woman in a while, but Bob just wants you to give his wife a message. Tell her that he's fine and he loves her. He also wants her to know that he felt no pain when he passed. He didn't suffer. He keeps pointing to his glasses and says he's giving them back to her."

Connie promised to track down her friend and pass on the message. I didn't understand the bit about the glasses, but sometimes you just have to relay what you hear. It may mean nothing to me, but it could mean the world to the one receiving it.

"Thanks, Connie. Now *you're* the medium," I said and smiled, noticing that once again the audience was sitting motionless and silent.

After the demonstration, Joe asked to see me before he returned to the hospital. He thanked me profusely, telling me that the entire family realized why they'd attended tonight and how much comfort they'd received at this extremely difficult time. Just knowing that Joe's mom wouldn't be alone when she passed was a relief for all of them.

"Don't thank me," I said. "The Sarge did all the work."

As tragic as endings can be, there's always a new beginning when it comes to the spirit world. In our bleakest of moments, it helps to know that the spirit isn't dwelling in the pain of the past, but remembering the love and warmth of those times with their loved ones on Earth.

chapter 15

LAUGHTER THROUGH THE TEARS

IT MAY SEEM LIKE THE CRAZIEST idea you've ever heard, but I'd like to make one thing perfectly clear: It's okay to find joy and even laughter in the spirit world. I know that we've been trained to view death as only a sad and somber affair, but I've linked with spirits who have a better sense of humor than some of us do.

So give yourself permission to be human in your loss, and embrace the laughter when you talk about (or to) your departed loved ones. You should remember these souls to their fullest, and what's better than hearing their laughter in your mind—even if it doesn't fill your ears anymore? They don't want you to hold on to sadness, but to go on with your life and embrace the happiness found here. Trust me on that one. By doing so, you'll be giving their lives on Earth the credit they deserve.

The following stories perfectly illustrate what I mean.

Spirit with a Sense of Humor

People often ask if we change at all after we pass over. I know that spirits progress and continue to learn, but basically whatever personality you had here is what you'll take with you when you leave the physical world. The body dies, but the mind and its consciousness goes on. This means that the personality and all its memories last forever. It's these personality traits that come through when I link—I can feel a spirit's essence, which I'm then able to relay to the client.

One particular reading I want to tell you about came from a woman named Doreen who made an appointment with me in the hopes of contacting her late husband. It turns out that she got an extra treat, because her departed mother also had plenty to say.

But let's start at the beginning. Doreen was referred to me by a friend who'd sat with me a year before. Doreen wanted to experience sitting with me as well, but she walked into my reading room looking a bit nervous. This was her first sitting, and she didn't know what to expect. I knew that talking to her for a minute or two would ease her nerves and allow me to start the reading.

We didn't need much small talk, because right away all lines of communication were open. So, I began. "Doreen, your mom has passed, correct?"

"Yes, she has," she stammered in surprise.

I wasn't shocked, because I'd known that her mom was there even before Doreen arrived. I said, "I feel her cancer along with her breathing problems, but she doesn't suffer any longer. She's calling out to your dad, which means he's still here."

Doreen nodded.

"You mom keeps saying, 'He's back, he's back.'"

"Dad just moved back to Massachusetts," she confirmed.

"Your mom's full of energy, and I can feel her upbeat personality. She keeps calling out the name Frank."

"That's my dad!" Doreen exclaimed.

"What's with the bell? Does someone collect them?"

"Well, my dad is older now, so when he wants something and can't get up, he'll ring a small bell."

"Tell him that Mom knows about the bell. Even she can hear it from where she is," I said with a smile. "I'm seeing flowers all around you, which means that an anniversary should be coming up this June."

"She passed in June," Doreen confirmed.

"She's telling me that her father is with her. He's the one who had the alcohol problem."

"You're absolutely right. He passed before her."

"Now she's calling out to her girls. You must have other sisters."

"Yes, I'm one of six girls."

"Your mom is sending her love to all her children, as well as her babies. I know she's talking about her grandchildren," I said. "Mom's showing me black-and-white photos. I'm not sure, but they look like acting and modeling stills to me."

"My mom's only granddaughter took dancing classes last year and had black-and-white professional headshots taken of herself," Doreen said in an amazed voice.

"Please tell her that Grandma's watching. Doreen, your mom is making me feel like she was semiconscious right before she passed on. But she wants to let you know that she was quite aware of everything that was going on around her. She knew that one of your siblings couldn't make it on the last night at the hospital. She wants you to tell them to let it go. There's no need to hang on to the guilt of not being there when she passed. Do you understand that?"

"Yes, one of my sisters couldn't get there in time."

"I keep hearing 'Florida,'" I said.

"That's where Mom lived, John."

"You're wearing her ring right now."

Doreen held up her hand to show me her mom's beautiful sparkling wedding ring. I paused for a minute because someone was interrupting us.

"Hang on, we're switching gears here. I keep hearing a name with a *P* and a *T* in it. . . maybe Peter?"

"My husband's name is Peter."

"He passed, yes?"

"Yes, I lost my husband a few years ago."

"Your mom says that she's with him, and she's also telling me that she had to be the first in line today when it came to saying hello to you. As you know, she was always the boss!"

Doreen started to laugh, acknowledging that her mom wore the pants in the family.

"Did your mom or husband call you 'Doe' as a nickname?"

"Yes, Peter did."

"This guy must have been a jokester, because he keeps giving me his sense of humor."

"Oh, yeah. He made everyone laugh," Doreen said, and she smiled when I told her that Peter was sending her a lot of love.

A moment passed, and I explained to her that I was seeing heart symbols. "Here comes Peter again. I can feel the shift in personalities. He's coming in much stronger—he really wants his turn now. In fact, he just bumped your mom for a moment. First off, he's thanking you for the garden."

"I did a beautiful flower garden in his honor."

"Did you do the garden at his grave or at your house? Oh, wait a minute. He just asked, 'How could she be at a grave when I was cremated?'"

"He *was* cremated!" she said as she shifted in her chair. "The garden is at our home."

"See, Doreen, he's good. No problem talking with this guy!" I chuckled to myself. "I can't tell you how much he's joking with me. Anyway, now he's showing me Niagara Falls."

"We went there together and had a great time."

"I have to admit that he's not talking much about how he passed."

"That's okay. Please go on," Doreen begged.

I gave her the next piece of evidence. "He's telling me to say 'Dee Dee.'"

Doreen giggled and told me that this was her sister's nickname.

"Did Peter and Dee Dee get along?" I asked.

"Yes, they loved to bust each other's chops," she said, laughing out loud and really enjoying this "reunion."

"I could tell, because he makes me feel like they had an ongoing humorous relationship. He's also saying that he cared for all your sisters, and he liked being surrounded by his 'girls.' This includes his mom, who's with him now."

Doreen nodded and told me that Peter's mom had passed before him.

"Well," I said, "now he has to deal with your mom *and* his. Peter says that his hands are full on the Other Side." I paused for a minute because Peter was suddenly becoming more serious. "He's telling me that whatever he passed from was found by accident during a routine visit to the doctor.

He keeps making me feel like there's fluid in the lungs or congestive heart failure."

"Yes, that's true," she said. "He was ill for a while and eventually passed from too much fluid around his heart."

"I can feel his weight loss, and he's telling me that he was quite strong before he got sick. When he found out that his body would no longer allow him to be independent, he didn't want that kind of life for himself or for you. I do believe that he chose to leave."

Doreen started to cry, confirming that Peter hated anyone seeing him ill or incapacitated because he considered himself to be a "man's man."

Looking into her eyes, I told her, "He wants to make sure that you know he's fine and he went peacefully in his sleep. He closed his eyes in this world and opened them in another. He's thanking you for keeping him in your life. You still talk to him, and he wants to let you know that he's receiving what you're telling him. Once again, he's joking with me. He just said, 'I really hear *everything*.'"

Doreen let out a laugh, knowing that she and Peter shared so much and always had great talks. Not only were she and Peter husband and wife, they were also best friends. She was glad that he was still hearing her when she'd whisper to him in the wee hours of the night.

Peter's spirit kept appearing to me—in fact, now he was twirling a pair of guns in his hands like a gunfighter. As I saw this image, I immediately said, "He really knew how to handle guns."

"Yes, he was a great marksman."

Switching gears, I asked, "Did Peter always bring you flowers?"

"Oh, yes!"

"Well, he's telling me that you should buy them for yourself now, so when you see them you'll remember that he's still with you." I paused because the next bit of information left me a bit perplexed. "Why am I hearing a loud chain saw? Did he cut his own wood for the fireplace?"

"Oh, God, yes! And he almost took down the house one time doing it!" Doreen was enjoying this sitting so much that I could see her joy reflected through the tears and laughter that went hand-in-hand in our conversation. She said that she felt Peter's energy right there next to her.

I confirmed that he was, in fact, right there by her side. His next message left me a bit confused, and despite our newly formed bond, I was a bit reluctant to pass it on to Doreen. So, I began with a tiny disclaimer: "I get a lot of information in my readings, and sometimes I can misinterpret what I receive, but I was trained to give what I receive." I went on. "I mean no disrespect in any way, but why is Peter talking about one testicle?" I held my breath waiting for her response—and hoping that she didn't slap me.

But Doreen was laughing so hard that she almost fell to the floor. Finally, she composed herself and answered my question. "John, he's saying one testicle because that's all he had! He had an accident when he was a kid."

Whew! I sighed with relief and said, "Well, that was a first for me! Of course, you know he's still joking about it." You see, when I do this work I'm actually talking to the spirit in my mind. When Peter was talking about that particular piece of evidence, I said to him, "I can't say that!" He came back and said, "No, say it! Say it! She'll understand. *Please!*"

Doreen's eyes twinkled. "John, I know that this is a very serious issue for some people, but it was always a joke with us. I wasn't expecting him to bring it up now, but who else but my Petey would say such a thing?"

"Okay. Your mom is back, and she's showing me a charm bracelet."

"I have that at home," said Doreen in a soft voice, and both of us knew that our time was coming to an end.

"Peter and Mom are fading now, and I'm losing their energy," I told her. "Peter says, 'I'll always watch your back.' Now he wants to make sure I say this properly. Here goes: 'I love you, babe!'"

"That's what he use to call me," Doreen responded. She touched her heart, looked to her side, and whispered, "I love you, too, babe."

She slowly got up from her chair, shaking her head in disbelief at what she'd just experienced. She thanked me, but I told her not to give me the credit—it was Peter who did most of the work.

Secretly, I'm thrilled that Doreen can smile when she thinks of Peter, knowing that her husband's charm and wit is still with both of them. She can also rest easy, knowing that her mom will keep an eye on him. Doreen left my office beaming, but it wasn't for me. She was smiling for Peter, and I know it was the type of grin he'd love.

The Puppeteer

Every single day in my job, I have what people call a "brush with greatness." I might be connecting with your mother or grandfather, and I don't care if they never did anything that made them famous during their time on this planet. In my book, the not-so-simple act of surviving a lifetime here is pretty spectacular stuff all by itself.

Having said that, I'd like to tell you about Marlena, a deep-voiced New Yorker who'd heard about my work from

Unsolved Mysteries and decided to pay me a visit. From the start, it was obvious that she was a professional woman— although I cautioned her not to tell me what she did for a living.

From the moment Marlena sat down, I was a bit confused. Immediately, I felt myself linking, and all I could see around her were hundred of feathers. I smiled, because I knew that the spirit world was playing with both of us—I certainly didn't think that Marlena had a farming background or worked in a pillow factory.

"Marlena, this might sound crazy, but what's with all the feathers? Plus, they're pink! You're going to have to help me out here because I don't know exactly what this means . . . except that maybe you're a Las Vegas showgirl in your spare time."

She laughed and said, "I haven't played Vegas, but he did."

He was the late Wayland Flowers, who performed with his puppet, Madam. Marlena filled in the blanks and told me, "Wayland always had feathers around him, and Madam wore them, too. I still have some, including the one I always carry with me." Marlena pulled out a small pink feather from her briefcase.

"You worked with him," I realized aloud.

She nodded and told me that for many years, she was Wayland's manager.

"I love this guy's energy," I said. "He's upbeat, he's laughing, and he's loud! I guess he hasn't changed at all. I know that the two of you had an unbelievable amount of joyful times when he was here. Together, you were an unstoppable team."

Marlena started laughing at the happy memories. "John, if we had a few years, I could tell you the stories."

"He knows how much you miss him, and he wants you to be serious for a moment, Marlena," I said. "He wants you to know that like your laughter, your love also doesn't die."

The smile slowly faded from Marlena lips, and I handed her a tissue.

"Right now he's telling me to thank you because you were one of the few who came to the hospital when he was so sick," I said, and then nodded as the information came quickly. "I'm getting that during that time, he saw some people who went before him and felt that they were coming to get him. Does that make sense?"

"John, I was at his bedside at one point, and he swore that he saw a white light in which his parents and grandparents were standing," she told me.

"I'm getting the feeling that someone else might have been sitting on the bed while you were there."

"No one believed me," she said, "but at one point, Wayland swore that he'd seen an angel sitting on the bed. He knew it was a female angel." She continued, "Later that afternoon, I checked with the hospital to see if any other women had been visiting Wayland that day. They showed me the sign-in log and confirmed that I was his only female visitor."

"That was his angel," I told her as Wayland passed on another message. "Speaking of which, he's glad that you liked the pin, and he wants you to stop worrying that it was too expensive. You're worth it!"

Marlena was speechless for several seconds. It turns out that a few months after Wayland passed, a mutual friend came to visit her, worried about Marlena because Wayland's death was obviously devastating. To Marlena, he wasn't just a client, he was a dear friend and a total original—no one could fill that void. She said, "My friend told me that she had a little gift for me, and handed me a tiny white box. It was an 18-karat-gold pin of an angel. I shook my head and said I certainly couldn't accept something that costly, but she just took the pin out of the box and secured it to my sweater."

"Marlena, even though I know your friend bought this beautiful pin for you, I feel that Wayland influenced her to buy it. It's almost as if it's from him."

Marlena looked thoroughly touched and amazed.

I went on. "Wayland has one more message for you: 'Enjoy the pin, and know that I'm watching over you.' He also wants me to remind you that his last wish was to do a Broadway show. He wants you to continue that dream and try to get there without him. He's telling me that if anyone can do it, you certainly can."

At that moment, I saw the pink feathers that were swirling around Marlena start to lift, as if they were being carried by a gentle breeze. "I think Wayland has another show to do tonight, and he's getting ready to take off," I told his manager, who looked at me with watery eyes.

"I wonder if God gets 10 percent as his new manager," she joked.

—— ◎ ——

chapter 16

HELP FROM THE OTHER SIDE

I'M FREQUENTLY ASKED IF SPIRITS watch us from the Other Side, and if they can still help us and influence our lives here. I've developed a standard reply, so here goes: They're not here to run our lives or tell us what to do, but spirits *can* guide us in the right direction. They can be with us when we need them the most, and we can lean on them as a source of strength and comfort. If they were here physically, they'd help, so why should it be any different now that they're not?

I got the opportunity to prove this one evening while lecturing on psychic awareness. In the crowd, I noticed the familiar face of a woman who had been to several of my events. As usual, she was sitting by herself in the back row. On this particular night, our time was coming to an end, so I opened up the floor to a few questions. Someone raised their hand and asked if their loved ones could still help them in this world. After giving my response and telling the audience how spirits can influence our lives, the woman tentatively raised her hand and asked if she could tell her story. I nodded yes, and the entire audience turned around to listen to her beautiful tale.

◉

Lisa had personally received help from the Other Side. Years ago, she'd been in love with a boy named Ned, and they were inseparable. One January evening, as Boston lay under a blanket of snow, the ground and the sky seemed to merge together as one gray blur. Lisa and Ned decided to stay home in the warmth of their apartment. They were enjoying the frigid evening by curling up together under a quilt and watching their favorite TV show. Neither wanted to cook, so they decided to order some take-out.

Lisa didn't have to protest too much when Ned volunteered to make a trek to a local restaurant to pick up their dinner order. He kissed Lisa, knowing how much she hated the cold, and said, "Stay right here, and I'll be back with our supper."

He never came back.

As Ned had made his way through the heavy snow, he'd crossed the main roadway and saw the lights of the restaurant about 50 yards in front of him. Picking up the pace, Ned had almost reached the curb, when, in the blink of an eye, a car came careening down the road. The driver never saw Ned, who was struck down and died instantly.

Later that night, Lisa had to make the worst call possible to Ned's parents.

Hundreds of friends attended the funeral, which was comforting, especially since there were some highly upsetting moments, too. At one point, Ned's mother walked up to

Lisa, looked at her straight in the eye, and told her that she blamed her completely for her son's death. She said that if Lisa had been with him, then maybe the tragedy could have been avoided.

Lisa was devastated by this verbal attack, and coupled with her own grief, the pain was almost too much to endure. It would take a long time to work through the loss, the feelings of guilt, and the waste of such a promising life. . . .

Eventually, Lisa met another wonderful man whom she later married. Two beautiful children were soon added to their lives. That should have been the end of her story, but it was actually just the beginning.

One night, Lisa had a dream of a young man with a radiant face who smiled at her. She forgot the dream . . . until it started to occur every night for weeks. It was the same man with the same smile who just stood there and never spoke to her. She started to realize that this man would have looked exactly like Ned if he'd been alive today, some 13 years later. Ned was 23 when he died that tragic evening, and he would have been 36 if he were still alive—which is how old this man looked.

The nightly visits in her dreams continued, and Lisa didn't know what to do except tell her husband. One night she had the strange feeling that she should immediately go visit a certain restaurant in her old neighborhood. She didn't understand where this sense of urgency was coming from or why she was being pulled to go there.

Lisa's husband was wonderfully supportive and suggested that she follow this path—no questions asked. Before Lisa could say another word, her husband was getting the kids out of bed and the car was packed.

It was more than 100 miles to her old neighborhood, and the closer they got to their destination, Lisa became more anxious. Suddenly, she spotted the take-out restaurant where her beloved Ned was heading that night he died, and she asked her husband to pull into the lot and park. She sat nervously in her car and asked her husband, "What should I do now?"

He looked into her troubled eyes, took her hand, softly stroked her face, and said, "Just go inside the restaurant and see what happens. There's a reason you keep seeing this face in your dreams, and a reason you felt the need to come here tonight."

Slowly, Lisa got out of the car, while her husband stayed with their sleeping children. After taking two steps into the restaurant, Lisa stopped dead in her tracks. In the far corner booth, she spied a man and a woman sipping coffee. For an instant, she was convinced that she recognized the woman sitting there. All sorts of thoughts were swimming around in her mind. *Could it be? It looks just like her. No, it couldn't be. Oh my God—it's Ned's mother.*

Lisa ran out of the restaurant crying, and her husband consoled her, helped her relax, and then said that she needed to go back in and speak with Ned's mother. He reminded her that there was a purpose for this trip, and she had to trust the results.

Lisa dug deep inside to gather the courage to leave the car again. But this time, she walked up to the table and introduced herself as Ned's old girlfriend. His parents looked up in shock as they clearly recognized Lisa. To her surprise, they asked her to sit down and join them.

In the next few minutes, Ned's parents explained that even though they now lived in another state, they were back in the area visiting some old friends. They had been on their way home when their car overheated. Strangely, this happened right outside this particular restaurant, and they decided to come inside for a cup of coffee while their car cooled down.

Ned's mother then became very quiet, and she started to weep. She took Lisa's hand in hers and begged for forgiveness, saying that she eventually realized that Lisa wasn't to blame for her son's passing. She admitted that she'd been so angry that she wanted to blame *someone* for taking her son away—Lisa was just the obvious choice. Over the years, Ned's mom had tried to find Lisa and apologize, but she didn't have any leads on her, due to the fact that Lisa had moved away and now had a different last name.

Lisa admitted that she'd been having dreams about a man who looked liked an older version of the Ned she remembered. Both women sat there holding each other as tears of forgiveness washed all the negative feelings away. For Lisa, the guilt she'd suffered for so long finally evaporated.

Lisa and Ned's mom agreed that in some inexplicable way, Ned had brought them together to help them in their healing process so that they could both go on with their lives.

As Lisa finished telling her tale, the audience applauded out of respect and to show how much they'd been touched by such a beautiful story. For Lisa, it was another form of release—and she knew that Ned was somewhere nearby, and he was smiling.

This type of communication is what's known as an ADC or After-Death Communication. People who have passed can and will help their friends and loved ones who remain here, and the spirits will do so in their own unique and special way. For instance, Ned must have been watching over and keeping an eye on both of these special women in his life for many years. He was a clever guy, because it took a lot of work to bring about this meeting.

Just think about it for a moment. Ned had to appear in Lisa's dreams over and over again to make her notice that this was no ordinary night of slumber. He even captured her interest by consistently showing himself as the same mature figure. And getting his parents to the restaurant and nudging Lisa at the same time to go to that specific place took a lot of juggling on his part.

Of course, I believe it helped that Lisa had a strong belief in the afterlife and an understanding husband. She knew that this was no coincidence—her long-ago love was playing the role of the peacemaker. He was also proving that the bonds of love established here can never be broken.

part III

your own
AWARENESS

INTRODUCTION

Psychic Foundation

WE'RE ALL BORN WITH SOME degree of psychic ability. The term *psychic* is actually Greek for "of the soul." Our psychic or intuitive senses are spiritual gifts, meant to assist us while our spirits are still in our physical bodies. They help us maintain our spiritual awareness and connection to the divine.

Few people realize that for every physical sense, there's a psychic sense that corresponds with it. For example, have you ever picked up the phone to call someone, and before you could even dial, you discovered that they were on the other end? Have you ever felt that urge to do something and then you decided not to—only to find that out you missed a great opportunity? Do you know when there's something wrong with someone close to you, even when they appear to be fine?

Well, here's the good news: *You're not crazy or different.* These incidents happen all the time, but we tend to ignore them, due to the fact that we're born into a world of science and technology that has moved us away from our own inner knowing or our psychic abilities.

In this section, I'll help you discover your own psychic abilities through various exercises that break down what I've learned. But first, I'd like to give you a little information about of what goes on when I'm onstage so you can begin to see how my mind works. Consider it the ultimate backstage pass, which might just help you to unfold your own awareness.

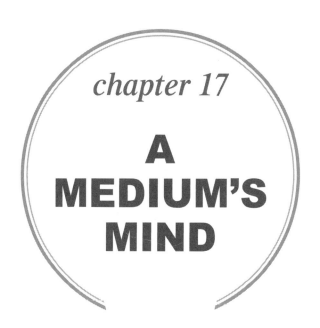

chapter 17

A MEDIUM'S MIND

BEFORE A DEMONSTRATION, I OFTEN like to make a connection to help me start off the evening. You see, even before I arrive at a lecture, I'm often aware of some spirit wanting to connect with their loved one. This usually means that they have a really strong personality and are using it to get my attention far in advance. One spirit even spent two hours "traveling" with me to a presentation. He was persistent for sure! But there are many times when I don't have any sort of link until the start of my mediumship demonstration. It's always different.

I'm frequently asked what I'm feeling or seeing during a link. It's a tough question, and I usually respond that you'd have to be in my mind to understand. Since I know that's impossible, I hope that this chapter will assist you when you're watching a medium work or when you go for a private sitting. Instead of just telling you about the messages

I receive, I want to take you through *some* of what happens to me during a demonstration.

The first thing you need to know is that I have no script when I walk onstage. Words come to me in the form of inspiration. I put my total trust in the spirit world to help me do my job. I know that I'm never alone on the stage; in fact, I'm often standing up there with a full cast of characters.

I call what happens a "three-way conversation," and it's a bit like a conference call between spirits, the members of the audience, and me. Each part has to be in sync to make a good connection and help the flow of information. It's not easy—I mean, it's hard enough to get three people in one room to agree on what to have for dinner!

Sometimes I walk out to see hundreds of faces in the audience, each one looking to me for hope and reassurance. I know that only a few will be chosen, but not directly by me. Some people sit there with their arms folded, jaws clamped tightly shut, and looks on their faces that say, "Prove it to me." I can *never* prove it to them. All I can do is give the best evidence I can by using my abilities, which have been fine-tuned through years of study and practice. Of course, there are those anxiously sitting on the edge of their seats, ready to grab on to anything I say in the hope that it's for them. My advice is: Don't *reach* for the evidence. Let the medium do his or her job.

I always state that when I do this work, it's as if I'm wearing my nerves on the outside of my body, because I'm overshadowed with the energy of the spirits. There was a time when I even started to do an Irish jig onstage because the spirit that I was linking with took step-dancing classes while he was here. The point is this: If a spirit want to get something across, they know what to do.

Someone once asked the great Scottish medium Albert Best if demonstrations of mediumship really convince the audiences who attend them. He answered, "We can't convince anybody of anything. We can only sow a seed. The greatest thing we can do is to stimulate people to find out more for themselves. We can't take away the pain of loss, but if we have taken away the fear of death, if we have given hope where there was none before, then we have done something worthwhile."

I couldn't agree more.

Before every demonstration, I always give a lecture to help educate the audience as much as I can on what mediumship is, and more important, what it isn't—I've found that many people who come to these events have little idea about the process. I talk about life after death; I also explain how I work as a medium so that the audience will find it easier to understand my signs and symbols during the demonstration. "Names will come through, and they don't have to be of someone who's passed," I'll say. "It can be someone who's living. Sometimes *you* may be the medium for someone else. For example, I could link with your friend's mother, for if the spirit knows that they can get a message through you to their people, trust me, they will."

I explain that when I link with spirits, I always hear them on my left; in fact, the audience will see me talking to spirits on that side of my body. (I always have to remember to prep the sound crew, too, or they'll think I have a stiff neck or something.) When I acknowledge the spirits, I often have to ask them to "speak louder, please." Or I'll say, "I don't understand what you're showing me."

One thing I like to underscore in my lectures is that mediumship is not an instant cure for the bereavement process. When someone passes, you must go through all the different stages of grief and deal with it in your own individual way. You need to confront all the emotions and feelings that surround your loss. In fact, if you tried to see me as soon as your loved one died, I'd refer you to a support group or a therapist instead. Until you've dealt with your bereavement, you shouldn't think about making a connection right away. Mediums can then assist in your healing process. (I also believe that the newly arrived spirit needs their own adjustment time before they're ready to send any messages.)

Most times, I try to keep the proceedings from getting too serious, although it *is* serious. Not everyone who attends a demonstration will get an individual message, so the lecture is my way of giving something to those people who won't get a personal connection. I pray that my words of encouragement, hope, and inspiration will give them something to remember.

These lectures vary according the crowd, the location, and how I feel when I walk out. I might talk about how the audience is still connected to their loved ones, offer words of spiritual guidance, or speak about how spirit communication works. All my lectures cover what I've said many times: "This is all about energy. Energy cannot die." Of course, I know that most people want me to demonstrate, not lecture, but I remain determined to mix both teaching and demonstrating.

No matter how we try to ignore them, spirits will make their presence known in one way or another. For example, during one demonstration I gave in Spokane, I received a strong link that I was convinced was for a woman in the fourth row. I pointed to her and asked, "Who's Jack?"

There was no response as she looked up at the ceiling searching her memory.

Once again, I repeated, "Who's Jack?" while still staring directly at her. "I have Jack here. He feels like an elderly gentleman, and says you should definitely know who he is."

Again, there was no response from this woman, so after a long pause, I tried again. "Darling, do you know a Jack who has passed?" This time, I almost shouted it into the mike, causing the entire audience to sit up straight.

"Well," she finally said, "my father's name was Jack, but he died 30 years ago. That's too long ago to come through."

The audience murmured in surprise, and I said, "But he's still dead, right?"

The woman nodded.

"Then he has the right to come through anytime," I gently told her. "If he's over there and wants to come to you, then it doesn't matter how long ago he passed."

Bless her—I think she finally got it.

I love to tell the audience how spirits will make themselves known no matter what—they can use dreams, make electricity dance, or move objects. I'll also say that if a picture of your late husband keeps tilting and you believe it may be your Bill, it may very well be . . . or you need to check the picture's hook. People want to connect so badly that they have a tendency to take *any* sign and believe it's from their loved ones. I'll tell them, "If I come to someone in the audience and bring through their beloved poodle, I don't want somebody else screaming out from the other side of the hall 'That's my cat!' A dog is a dog and a cat is a cat—it's that simple."

Another problem is people's lack of knowledge about their family history. That's why it's helpful to do a little research before seeing a medium. *Anyone* can come through.

There are times when I'll come to someone in the audience, and they can't acknowledge the evidence. Other times, I'll get an e-mail the next day, saying, "John, I understood what you were bringing through, but I was too nervous to raise my hand. What was the message?" Sadly, I can't go back and pick up where I left off. The phone has been hung up and the communication has been lost. It takes a lot of energy for spirits to come to us, and I get frustrated when I see it wasted.

I refer to myself as the "drawbridge": I raise my energy, and the spirits lower theirs. A bridge is then built, and using the power of love, we have a connection that flows with feelings, words, and memories.

I always feel the quickening increase as the spirits draw closer. At certain points, several of them vie for my attention, and it can get quite raucous in my head. But one night I was having trouble linking before a demonstration. Right before I was to go on, I suddenly started picturing Big Ben in London. Obviously, this was a spirit communication coming through. "Finally, you guys!" I muttered. "You're a little late tonight!"

I knew that this would be my first link for the evening. I often tell people that I "hear the pictures." It's as though I see a picture or a scene and know everything that goes with it—as if there are some unseen words attached to the image.

On this particular night, I stood at the side of the stage, and was immediately aware of the rest of "the cast" who had gathered around me. I heard the final few words of welcome from the announcer and began walking up the steps as the auditorium was filled with the words: "Ladies and gentlemen, please give warm welcome to a very special man—John Holland."

I was on!

It's always strange to walk onstage and hear hundreds of voices suddenly become silent. This felt like a good crowd, even if I couldn't see them all. "Good evening, ladies and gentleman," I said. "When I was walking in this evening, I walked by two women looking at my brochure, and I heard one of them say, 'You know, Helen, he looks so normal.'"

The audience roared with laughter. I deliberately told this joke to raise the energy level in the room and help people relax. A little humor always breaks the ice. I went on: "I'm not sure what people think mediums are supposed to look like. I left my cape and turban back at the house!"

After I delivered my preliminary lecture, I glanced into the audience, knowing where I was supposed to start. I could feel my Big Ben link coming in stronger. "I'm coming to the back of the room, and I believe that this message belongs to someone in the very last row," I announced.

My runner for the night, a young woman in sneakers who handled the mike, began to hightail it all the way back there to make sure the entire audience could hear the responses.

"Is there someone sitting at the back associated with London, or is someone going to London soon?" I asked.

Immediately, a pair of hands went up.

"Do you ladies understand London?" I inquired, while the pace inside me was quickening, causing me to talk faster and faster.

"Yes! Yes! We're going next week," the women answered almost in unison.

"Thank you. Which one of you has the mom who's passed over from cancer?" I asked them.

"I do," said one of them.

"I have her here, and she's thanking your friend next to you for bringing you here this evening." Meanwhile, the mother was chattering in my head. "She's telling me that you'll love London, and she's quite excited about it. Who has the *J* name?"

"I do. My name is Janice," the woman replied.

"Well, Janice, Mom is sending her love to all the family and especially to your sister. Do you understand this?"

"Yes," she said, crying tears of joy. This confirmed that her mom was still watching and that Janice would be able to enjoy the trip that she and her mom had always planned to take together. Somehow, I thought her mom would still be going with her, except she wouldn't need to buy a ticket!

I felt another spirit take over. I was being pulled to the very front of the audience, and I began to see surgical stitches on someone's lower back. I started to focus on three rows back and to my right.

"Who in this area understands having problems with their lower back or perhaps has just had a back operation?" I asked.

A woman raised her hand and said, "My dad had a back operation this past week."

I asked the spirit for more information. What came back was an intense feeling of a mother's love. "I feel like your mom has passed, and she's showing concern for her husband. Do you understand this?" I asked the woman.

She looked shocked, and said, "Yes, I do."

"Your mom is thanking you for taking care of your dad and watching him so closely," I said. "She knows he has trouble staying in one spot for very long, and she wants you to know that he's getting up while you're at work."

The woman laughed and said, "That's definitely how my dad is!"

"Now your mom is telling me that her passing was fast and unexpected. She had no time to say good-bye properly, but she wants you to know that in her heart, she was saying that she loved you," I said.

As the woman struggled to form her words, I started to see my symbol for a medical connection. "Who's the nurse?" I continued.

"Mom was, and so am I," she said.

"Your mom wasn't here to see you graduate, but she knows you're a nurse, and she's so very proud of you."

The woman was openly weeping now. She said, "On my way here, I asked her to please come through if she was able to do so. As a sign, I asked her to mention the nursing so that I'd know it was her."

"Well, darling, I guess your mom heard you loud and clear. Take her love and know that she's right there with you. And don't forget what she said about your dad—he's hard to keep down."

The audience applauded, showing their support. But it was time for me to move on again.

I was being pulled away from the front because "Betty" was being called out to me. I was forcibly drawn to the right side of the hall. Before I knew what I was saying, I heard myself calling out, "Betty! Betty! Betty! I'm hearing the name Betty being called to the back of the room on the right-hand side."

I saw two hands cautiously dart into the air, and as the mike was being passed to them, I asked, "Do you ladies understand the name Betty?"

"Yes, that's our mom," said one woman.

Now I heard two names. "Is there another Betty or an Elizabeth?"

"Yes! Our grandmother is Elizabeth, and her daughter is our mom, Betty," said the other woman.

Meanwhile, the audience seemed mesmerized as all eyes focused on the two women. *Their* eyes were fixed on *me* as I paced across the stage. This link was incredibly strong. "Okay, ladies, I feel like I have your grandmother here, and she's telling me that you two are her granddaughters, but your other sister isn't here tonight."

"Yes!" they said in unison. "She doesn't go for this stuff."

"Well," I replied, "please tell her that Grams says hi!" Deep down, I knew I wasn't linking with a Betty Crocker-type grandmother. What the audience wasn't seeing or feeling was this woman's zestful energy and wit.

"Your grandmother feels very youthful to me, and she wants to be known as 'the cool grandmother,'" I said with a smile. Both sisters just kept grinning and nodding their heads. "Can this be right?" I asked in an amazed voice. "I'm seeing a pair of white go-go boots! Ladies, your cool grandmother is showing me her favorite thing to wear back in the '60s. Please tell me you understand that one!"

Once again, the audience laughed, and all eyes turned to the sisters. One of them said, "Our grandmother was a model, and we have some photos of her wearing her best '60s gear, including her white go-go boots!"

"Well, I did say she was cool!" I responded, as the audience applauded in delight. Surrounded by the intense love between the generations, I continued. "Your Grams is coming through like a second mother, but she wants to make sure that you say hello to your mom."

As I was losing the link, I added, "Ladies, this was your grandmother's opportunity to say hello to her family. She's fine and will always be watching and sharing in all of your lives. Grams is a very clever lady and an awesome communicator. It was my pleasure to be the middleman for you both. Please take her love, and make sure you tell your mom about the boots."

The sisters held each other, giggling and chatting.

I could feel the spirit world drawing back, and my pace was slowly coming back to normal. "The door to the Other Side will be closing soon, but just for tonight," I told the crowd, who moaned because it was almost "a wrap."

"Thank you, ladies and gentleman, for coming this evening," I said. "If you didn't get a message tonight, it doesn't mean they're not there. I'm not in control of who gets the messages—*they* are. Please know that your loved ones are *all* safe and still with you. And I'd like to encourage you to tell the people who are in your lives now how much you love them and know how precious *every* moment with them here is. Always remember, those on the Other Side are only a thought away. Good night everyone, and God bless."

At the end of this special evening, I hoped that those who attended would go back to their lives with a sense of comfort and peace, knowing that we all survive death and we're never truly alone.

I feel so lucky when a connection is made and understood. In a way, I'm part of a wonderful reunion. I get to share in the memories, and most of all . . . the love.

— ◎ —

chapter 18

FREQUENTLY ASKED QUESTIONS

DURING MY LECTURES, I USUALLY open the floor to questions, since people love to ask me about spirituality, mediumship, love, life, death, dreams, reincarnation, and so forth. I can only go by my own experiences and what I've studied. Therefore, it's important to stress that the answers I provide are my personal opinions and beliefs.

Throughout my career as a medium, I've kept a list of the questions I'm most frequently asked. I hope that you'll find some answers to the things you've been wondering about.

Q. Where is the spirit world?

A. It isn't above us or below us—it's all around us. You see, everything is made up of energy and vibrations. The vibrations of this world are slow and dense, whereas the spirit world vibrates at a much higher rate. That's why it's invisible to the human eye. There's a thin layer between this world and the next, and the only thing that separates us is the frequency of the vibrations.

Q. Can anyone become a medium?

A. Many times I've heard the line "mediums are born and not made." That said, let me add that *everyone* is born with a degree of psychic ability, and each and every one of us has the capability to improve and develop our awareness. And we can all connect with our loved ones who have passed, through the power of thought and through our dreams. I've said many times that they're "only a thought away." We can assist them in contacting us by learning to increase and raise our energy— by doing so, we'll help in the communication by meeting them halfway.

If you have the gift of mediumship, it will present itself in its own way and in its own time. To actually practice as a working medium takes dedication, patience, and time; and it can be a physically demanding job. This undertaking is not to be taken lightly. Mediumship has to develop and grow; you'll find that most mediums spend their entire lives developing their abilities. You must also be ready to live a life of service.

Q. When it's my turn to cross over, will it matter what religion or faith I practiced?

A. Most religions have some belief in the afterlife— some more than others. I do believe that it helps to follow some kind of faith, for with its teachings, it can assist us when it's our time to cross over. I like to use the analogy of the spokes of a wheel: Each spoke represents a different religion or faith, and although each is independent of the other, they're all moving in the same direction.

We're all born with the spark from the divine (our spirit), so when our spirit crosses over, that spark will leave the "jacket" it's encased in and move back into the spirit world where we all originated from. We all survive death, no matter what (if any) religion we choose to believe.

Q. Are there bad spirits, and if so, do they come to you?

A. In all the years that I've done this work, I've yet to have a malevolent spirit or energy link with me. I strongly believe in the saying "like attracts like": I work for the highest good, consider myself a child of God, and believe in a Higher Power; therefore, I wouldn't attract this type of energy. Instead of calling them "bad spirits," I'd rather refer to them as spirits that exist at a lower vibration and dwell in the lower spheres of the spirit world. They're just farther away from the Divine Source, so it will take a longer time for them to reach a higher level.

Q. Are there different levels in the spirit world?

A. Most definitely. Every lesson and deed here determines what level you'll go to when you leave this physical world. You're incarnated into a physical body to assist you in your soul's growth, which is why it's so important to try to be the best you can be while you're here. You should continually strive to be compassionate and kind, and give assistance and love to others. This will always increase your rate of vibration. And when it's your time to pass, your spirit will gravitate to its rightful level.

Q. Are the spirits connected to us all the time?

A. Your family and friends here in the physical world aren't around you 24/7, but they can be with you if you need them—it's the same way with your family and friends on the Other Side. People don't realize how much energy it takes for those who have passed to lower their vibration and make a connection to this physical plane, so it's not something they want to be doing all the time. In addition, I believe that they have their own learning to do over there and need time to grow and progress, which is why those who have recently passed often need time before they'll connect to the living.

Q. Why do spirits come back?

A. Because they can. People on the Other Side want to share our lives with us. I've done many sittings where spirits acknowledge that they were around their loved ones during difficult times to lend their support and strength. However, they don't just visit when the going gets tough. I often receive evidence of spirits who were there to see their child get married or witness the birth of a baby. Holidays and special occasions are also big for them—they want to see us happy and like to take part in that joy. After all, if they were here physically, they'd be at such events. Being in spirit doesn't change the fact that they're still our family and still care about us.

Q. Can they help from the Other Side?

A. Like those dwelling here, they can assist you, send you love and support, and even inspire you; however, it isn't their job to tell you what to do, or to do it for you. *You* have to make your own decisions and take responsibility for your choices and actions. They can't interfere with the lessons you need to learn while you're here.

I remember a woman who was thrilled that her mother came through during our session. She wanted her mom to tell her if she should divorce her husband. Of course, the mother couldn't make that decision for her because it wasn't her job. The woman needed to take responsibility for her own life.

Q. Do people change when they cross over?

A. Each time I link with spirits, they appear to be exactly the same as they were here. People seem to think that those who pass somehow turn into these exalted beings, yet they have the same personality and quirks on the Other Side. They're still upbeat, humorous, strict, or relaxed over there. However, I do believe that spirits progress over time and raise themselves to a higher level.

It means a lot to my clients when I blend with their loved ones and start to describe and take on their personality or some of their individual habits. Since we're all so different, getting a spirit's personality can sometimes be the best evidence for a client.

Q. Can you still communicate with my parents even if they didn't speak English?

A. Yes. My type of mediumship works on a mental level. I receive images and words through the power of thought, so there's no language barrier. I've read for Ethiopians, Asians, Latinos, Brazilians, and many more. Each time I connect with someone who has lived in another country, I always feel their culture and understand their experiences. It's almost as if I'm actually there. Sometimes I may even come up with a word or saying in their language that I've never spoken before.

Q. Can you give us your views on suicide?

A. There's no running from your problems: Since there's no real death, there's no escape from your dilemmas or issues. I've linked with many people who have taken their own lives, and I get a very different feeling when I'm communicating with them. They're usually full of regret because they can see how those left behind are affected. On the Other Side, they may be shown the difference they could have made in their own lives as well as the lives of others if they'd chosen to stay.

When these spirits communicate with me, they rarely want to talk about how they passed, and they never link with me for very long. Usually someone who's passed before them, such as a family member or friend, will come forward to help with the communication. I believe that these spirits need all their energy to work on themselves and are going through a process of healing.

I always tell people that prayer can help those on the Other Side who have taken their own lives, and in this way, they can be assisted in the healing process.

Q. Do you call the dead to you?

A. No. Just like us, spirits have free will—mediums don't have power over them. Usually you'll hear from the ones you hope will communicate, but no medium can ever guarantee who will come through. Some people who have sat with me want to connect with a certain person, but end up hearing from someone they never expected. It isn't a case of 1-800-Dial-the-Dead.

For example, I once visited a client named Vivian who wanted to sit with me but had trouble walking. I agreed to go to her home, and she put me in her mother's room, sat me in her chair, and even made sure her mom's photos were all around me. Did she get her mother? You guessed it—no. But a woman did come through for Vivian—a friend of hers. As I started to describe her to Vivian, she screamed, "What do you want?!" while looking up at the ceiling.

It turns out that ever since Vivian had lost her mom, she'd been a recluse. Her friend came through to say that she was with her and wished she'd visit her other friends.

Q. Do animals exist in the spirit world?

A. Absolutely. We're all part of God's creation—each and every living being has a spirit, and that also goes for the four-legged kind. All kinds of animals come through: I've had dogs, cats, lizards, and even parrots that chose to sit on his owner's shoulder. Often someone who has passed will come through with their beloved pet or acknowledge that your furry friend is by their side and being taken care of by them. All animals survive on the Other Side.

Q. How do you feel about reincarnation? And is my loved one there for me the moment I cross over?

A. I totally believe in the process of reincarnation, which is just one of the many metaphysical subjects I've studied. Almost all of the research that I've read indicates that we reincarnate every 200 years or so, but I believe that there's some free will involved in the process: Some may choose to come back much sooner, and the rule is that each life is an individual process.

Many people have told me that they feel as though they've known someone they've just met. They sense a familiarity, as if they've known each other their entire lives. These days, much research and investigation is being done with people who have remembered their past lives and can actually find the evidence to back it up. For instance, I have a friend named Valerie who spoke French in her sleep from the ages of three to five. Her mom just thought she picked up a few words from TV, but when she started to speak in actual sentences, her mom had no idea where she could have learned this language. No one in the family had ever spoken French. Eventually, Valerie stopped speaking it, probably because she started to forget her past life.

From what I understand, we can reincarnate with the same group of people over and over again—each taking turns playing different roles. Think about it: Have you ever seen a child who seems to be the parent in the relationship? It could be that at one time, he or she *was* the parent!

As for the last part of the question, I can easily say yes. Your loved ones will be right there for you when it's your turn to cross over.

Q. Are guides and angels the same thing?

A. In my experience, a spirit guide has lived at some time or another on Earth in a physical body, while an angel has never had a physical incarnation. Every medium has one or more guides who work with them—some are constant and some change during the medium's life, but each has their own unique influence over the development of the medium's gifts. (As I've already mentioned, I have three of them.) But many people have these guides, not just mediums. They may show themselves in many forms, such as a Franciscan monk, an indigenous person, an ancient Egyptian, or even a child. I believe that they choose to show themselves in these familiar forms for our benefit. I feel that too many people place responsibility on these guides and expect them to do the person's work. Guides are here to assist, not make decisions.

Angels are in a totally different category than guides—they're "Messengers of God." There are thousands of people from many different cultures who have had experiences with these beings. According to ancient Jewish tradition, angels were the first intelligent beings, created by God to help sustain life and assist us in all areas of our lives. Have you ever said to yourself, "How did I get out of that situation safely? It must have been luck." Well, luck *may* have come into it, but more than likely, you had a little angelic assistance.

I remember being in a parking garage in Los Angeles, and I was driving up a steep incline. Another car came flying over that hill in the opposite direction, coming right at me with lightning speed. All of a sudden, my car stalled right in its tracks. Had I continued to drive, I would have hit the approaching car head on, but because my car stopped so suddenly, the other car had room to avoid me. Was it just luck that my car chose to stop at that exact time . . . or did I have a little help? I think I know the answer to that one.

Q. How can I be more spiritual?

A. Being spiritual is more than just taking a workshop or reading a book—*it's a state of mind.* How we live, what and how we think, and helping others in need is all part of being spiritual. We're always given the opportunity to raise our vibration to a higher level simply by our actions. So many people are trying to have spiritual experiences when the truth is simple: We're spiritual beings trying to have human experiences. Acts of unconditional love and compassion are the highest forms of "being spiritual." Each and every one of us is capable of such wonderful and beautiful things. We can achieve so much with our time here, so let's embrace it!

chapter 19

LESSONS FOR LIFE

PEOPLE ASK ME ALL THE TIME how they can learn to become more psychic. My answer is simple: Take it one step at a time and begin to learn the mechanics that lay the foundation for your awareness to unfold.

In this chapter, I'll break down the specific components of my training at Stansted so that you, too, can learn the basic mechanics of psychic awareness.

Meditation and Breath

At Stansted, we began each day with a meditation accompanied by the strains of soft music. I had to train myself to still my mind and let my thoughts drift in and out without dwelling on them. It isn't easy to control the thinking process in this way—at least not at first. But after much practice, I learned to watch information pass through my mind as if it were gentle, flowing water. Magically, I found that the more I meditated, the more the chatter in my mind diminished. To this day, I use meditation to find my own spirit in the much-needed silence.

When that silence is achieved, the spirit people are able to make their thoughts and feelings known to me. Meditation (which we'll also delve into in the next chapter) takes discipline, but it's a wonderful way to help anyone discover the reality of the soul and its independence from the rest of the body.

Learning the importance of proper breathing techniques can also deepen the meditative state. Through different breathing techniques, I've learned how to alter my consciousness. But it took a while for me to realize the importance of breath work. It's sounds strange, but most of us don't breathe properly. I recommend that you learn the art of breathing rhythmically and deeply. To do this, you must study what yogis call the *complete breath*. This is the proper way of breathing from the stomach, into the lower chest, and finally into the upper chest. If you watch a baby breathe, you'll notice that's what they do.

At Stansted, we were taught that "breath is life and life is the breath." The study of breath is truly a science in itself, and many books have been written on the subject. They're worth investigating, because breathing correctly can change your life forever. The book *Science of Breath* by Yogi Ramacharaka is a wonderful guide.

Blending and Linking

I was taught two very special concepts at Stansted, which are fundamentals of establishing contact with the deceased. First, when we *blend* with someone who has passed, our energy combines with theirs. Once this process is established, we now have a *link*—that is, words or images start to form in our mind, and the connection has been established.

Our tutors wanted to make sure that we thoroughly understood the concept, so they impressed upon us that everything is made up of energy. We're in a world of spinning atoms and molecules that are constantly vibrating. No matter what happens, energy does not die—it simply transforms. This means that every living thing, in its most basic form, is just pure energy.

To help us practice the process, the tutors taught us to feel each other's energy by placing us in chairs facing each other . . . blindfolded. We had to reach out with our minds and expand our energy fields to see if we could feel whether the person in front of us was male or female or whether we could pick up their emotions. This was a great benefit to me, because I realized that mediumship is just blending and linking with energy that's no longer tied to a physical body.

I'm reminded of a saying I once read by Paramahansa Yogananda: "We are electrical beings with intelligence." Therefore, if you think about yourself as energy, it will help you stay grounded and not get confused by a subject that many people take to the extreme.

The Power of Thought

Most people don't realize that thoughts are made up of energy, too—be it positive or negative. Anytime you think a particular thought, your aura will magnify it with energy and put it out to the universe; and so, *everything* in the material world starts off as a simple thought. One of my favorite sayings is: "Energy goes where action flows." In other words, if you put action into creating your thought, and if it's for the highest good, then it will manifest itself into reality (For example, seven years ago I was walking through a bookstore, and I imagined this book on the shelf. I kept that as an active thought, and eventually the book was written.) Think about what you want the most and picture it happening. In this way, you'll put the thought out to the universe.

Thoughts are powerful things, so take special care with what you put out there. We have to accept personal responsibility for *all* our thought and actions—there's no way around it. Keep this universal law in mind: "What you sow, you also reap." Never were truer words spoken. For instance, how you think about someone, and the thoughts you have about them, can have a significant effect in your relationship with that person. When dealing with other people, try to remember that they're always a reflection of you. Try to see the divine in everyone you come in contact with. In doing so, good can—and will—be reflected to you.

Psychometry

Psychometry is the practice of holding someone's personal possession and then "reading" the object, almost as if you were somehow seeing through touch. Remember that everything is made up of energy, including your favorite ring, the shirt you might be wearing, or that old chair—and they're all tools for a psychic. Have you ever borrowed someone's jacket and it made you feel different? You're picking up that person's emotions and their essence.

At Stansted, we used flowers to practice this technique. We weren't told which classmate brought in a specific flower—all the flowers would be arranged in a vase, and we'd have to choose the ones that we associated with each student. This was an excellent way to train our abilities, and with more practice, it would prove invaluable in helping us establish a strong link with someone in spirit. It was as if holding a beautiful blossom was a way to open the doors to another world.

Psychometry can help you reach beyond your five physical senses by tuning down your conscious mind and reaching a psychic level. Even when someone gives you a contract or business card, you can learn how to interpret what that other person is feeling—positive or negative—and this can help you make the right business decision. Psychometry can lay a good foundation for psychic work, and I recommend it if you're interested in developing your own abilities. It will help you *see* with your hands.

Try it for yourself: Hold something that has special meaning for another person. Write down the first few things that come to mind, and then share them with the owner of the object. You might be amazed by the way your feelings translate into facts.

Symbology and Colors

We live in a visual world with symbols and colors everywhere. Some psychics and mediums rely purely on symbols when sitting with their clients. Many of my symbols have changed over the years, while others have always remained constant. I always remember what one tutor told us: *"The soul never thinks without a mental picture."*

Through our dreams, symbols are pushed into our conscious mind from our subconscious. I encourage you to keep a dream journal, so you can keep a record of different symbols and what they mean to you. Everyone is different, so not all symbols mean the same thing to everyone.

Colors have unique energy patterns as well as their own frequencies, which affect you in profound ways. Certain hues will make you feel certain ways. In my psychic awareness class at Stansted, we'd try to guess what colors were on different cards based on whether the cards felt hot or cold. We also experimented with various forms of drawing and painting, letting the colors influence and heighten our senses. We'd also have students from different classes stand in front of us, and just by psychically going into their space, we'd tell them what color their aura was and what color they needed in their life. For example, red means energy, blue is for calmness, green is to assist in healing, and gold is for protection.

But colors, like symbols, can mean different things to different people. Only *you* can decipher what they really mean to you.

Receiving the Information

Each of us has five physical senses to help us in the physical world. But, as I've mentioned before, for every physical sense, there's a psychic inner sense that goes with it. I might see, feel, or even hear through my psychic senses. Sometimes I can even taste and smell with my abilities.

You might be stronger in one area than another. If you're a good "feeler," then you should work to strengthen that ability before you try to move on to your other senses. Often beginners think that seeing is the best way to receive information, when in fact, being a good feeler can produce dramatic results. In time, all the psychic senses may come together and work in unison. Try to discover and work with *your strength,* which is the way to begin to build a solid foundation with your psychic self.

Clairvoyance: Clear Seeing

This is when you receive images, pictures, symbols, and colors. You might also be sent information on how the spirit looked when he or she was here. Clairvoyance is often missed because the images are very quick and fleeting, and you have to give off the information as fast as it comes in. You're using your inner eye (better known as "the third eye"). Picture your kitchen in your mind's eye: Can you see it? Many psychics and mediums see this way. If you've ever watched a medium or psychic, you've probably noticed that we have a tendency to look away or over the shoulder of a client. We're not being rude—we're looking onto a screen (which I call the "psychic screen") with our third eye. It's almost as if a movie is playing out right in front of us.

Being aware of this phenomenon can help you in your study of psychic matters. And any meditation or guided-visualization exercise will enhance and sharpen your clairvoyant abilities—just make sure to practice!

Clairaudience: Clear Hearing

This is the ability to hear names, dates, certain sayings, and even songs. When hearing *subjectively,* (in your own mind), you're hearing words in your own voice. But some people hear *objectively,* which is outside of themselves. Have you ever heard your name being called and no one was there? It may be from a spirit or it could be someone who's thinking of you here. Try calling that person up and say hi. Most likely they'll say, "I was just thinking of you."

Also, if you hear a song playing in your head, try to notice what song it is. Listen closely to the words—there could be a message of encouragement or advice for you or someone else who needs a little upliftment.

Clairsentience: Clear Feeling

Basically, this is your inner sense of knowing. Most psychics and mediums are good feelers. We sometimes feel illnesses, aches, pains, and all ranges of emotions. We don't take on those symptoms because the spirits are just giving us memories of what they had while they were here in the physical world.

Some people can walk into a room and simply feel if an argument took place there. Why? The energy is still in that room. Or let's say that you're introduced to someone and you immediately have an uneasy feeling. It's not so hard to grasp what you're feeling—you're picking up thoughts and feelings from that person in your solar plexus area, which is felt through clairsentience. This explains the expression we all use so often: "I had a gut feeling about. . . . "

Write down these gut feelings or talk about them with those around you. Pay attention to see how often you're right or even correctly predict something. It's an interesting exercise at the very least, and you might confirm your own sense of "knowing."

The Chakras

The word *chakra* is an Indian word meaning "wheel." I like to refer to chakras as "spiritual batteries": centers for reception and transmission of physical and psychic energy within and around the body. We *all* have them. There are seven major chakras in the body, which run upwards along the spine and correspond to particular endocrine glands. They're the portals between the physical and spiritual realms. When I lecture, I always say, "Our bodies are like one big psychic antenna—find out how the equipment works."

I spoke about chakras in Chapter 4 when I had my automobile accident. During the crash, I experienced what's known as a "Kundalini Awakening"—all my centers were opened at once and very quickly, which caused me to have rushes of energy up and down my body. Let me explain why.

Each chakra corresponds to the spiritual gifts you're using. For example, the third-eye chakra helps with clairvoyance, the throat chakra assists in clairaudience, and the solar plexus chakra is associated with clairsentience. Each chakra is associated with a certain color and even resonates with its own individual musical tone. I'm sure you've seen people chanting, but what's actually happening is that they're tuning up their entire chakra system. Using their voice, they chant to stimulate and spin each one.

Whereas people in Eastern cultures know about chakras from birth, here in the West, we've only just begun to study these amazing spiritual batteries. Please research the chakra system—you'll learn so much about the energies in and around your body, and how they help you to be here in the physical world. I recommend that you read *The Wheel of Life* by Anodea Judith to learn more.

Inspiration

One afternoon in Spirit Boot Camp, we were informed that it was time to give an inspired speech on an unrehearsed subject. To be "put on the spot" in this way, we had to connect with Spirit and be inspired by our guides. To practice this technique, we had to choose a card with one word printed on it; then we'd talk about the subject to the group for several minutes.

When it was my turn to reach in and pull a card, I chose the card that said "gift." I simply closed my eyes and felt Spirit draw close. I tried to put my own thoughts aside as I created space in my mind. I relaxed and didn't analyze the words that came out of my mouth, which were: *"Your gifts are like a rose unfolding. You cannot force the bloom. When the rose is opened, then and only then will you feel it, smell it, and finally, touch it."*

My tutors and fellow students knew that I'd succeeded, because I certainly don't talk that way (although I wish I did!).

You can try this on your own or with friends by putting several words into a hat and then giving an unrehearsed speech on the one you pick. The first few times you try it, you might draw a blank—or you might find yourself waxing poetic on a subject that's foreign to you. Just speak from your heart, let your guides assist you, and tap in to the inspiration you feel at that exact moment you draw the card. More often than not, wonderful things will happen.

Telepathy

Husbands and wives or long-time partners are known to finish each other's sentences or speak the same words at the same exact time. We laugh when this happens and call it a coincidence, but that's not always the case. How can we explain how family members often know when something's wrong with one another? Or why is it that certain people simply think of someone they haven't seen in a long time and then will "run into them" later that day? This is no random bit of luck. It's actually what's known as *telepathy,* or the ability to send and receive messages and information through the mind. The energy of thought is a spiritual power, and I believe that what fuels this ability is love.

Communication and closeness with departed loved ones is possible without seeing a medium. So many people come to see me and long to connect with the Other Side when, in fact, they'll be receiving the information secondhand. To experience your *own* communication firsthand, simply realize that when you're thinking of those who have gone on before you, it could be because—*at that exact moment*—they're lovingly thinking of you, too. Be aware of each time you think of them and keep an open mind. (You can also write in a journal to record these thoughts.)

I heard a story once about a child's belief in the power of thought that illustrates my point perfectly. It revolves around a little girl named Daisy who passed on at the very young age of ten. During her last days, Daisy looked up and told her mother that she was communicating with her little brother who had passed years earlier. In fact, Daisy told her mother that the little boy was standing right beside her and the two were having quite a lively conversation.

"How do you speak to your little brother? I don't hear or see you moving your lips," asked the bewildered mother.

The grinning little girl answered, "We talk with our think."

chapter 20

FINE-TUNING YOUR AWARENESS

THERE HAVE BEEN MANY BOOKS written on spiritual unfoldment and developing one's awareness. I recommend that you research and experiment to find out what really works for you. The following techniques have worked for me and have psychically jump-started many of my students. Take your time, have patience, and enjoy the process.

Meditation Exercises

As I mentioned in the previous chapter, I've found that the art of meditation (along with breath work) can be one of the most beneficial ways to begin your journey into awareness. I find that meditation allows me to *look* at a problem or situation instead of being *in* it. It's a chance to stand back and view an issue with new eyes and a new understanding. There's a saying I love, which goes: "They say when you pray, you're talking to God, but when you meditate, you're talking with God." Meditation just might be the spiritual window you need to open yourself to a whole new world.

The word *meditation* for some brings to mind a guru chanting atop a mountain or a monk sitting alone in a cave. Meditation is simply a state of being in which the active mind slows down. It will bring you to a place where you can shut down your mental chatter and become more aware of the subtle energies inside of you.

We strive for financial success, good jobs, nice cars, and all those material things we think we need. These are all fabulous, but they're not the ultimate answer. When we reach for things outside of ourselves, we often move farther and farther away from our spark or life force. The most important thing in life is to *feed our soul* and try to maintain a balance.

We must learn to pull way back from the strains of daily life and go within to find that peace. Meditation can do that for us. It can also produce great health benefits. For instance, the relaxation and calmness that comes from meditating can enhance the immune functions of the body, reduce blood pressure, increase physical energy, and assist in your overall well-being.

Now let's be honest. You may have the best intentions to start your meditation practice, but life will try to stop you. That's why you have to make an effort to devote time to this practice. Try starting with just 15 minutes each day. Soon you'll learn to increase the length of your meditation, and you'll look forward to your special time with yourself and your spirit.

So many people think that meditating means that you must force your mind to go blank. That's impossible. However, you *can* learn to watch your thoughts come in and go right out again. Soon, these same thoughts will no longer have any power over you.

The meditation below is one that I use in my workshops because it's a great introduction to the process. I find that it helps to do it the same time every day, whether in the early morning or in the evening. Let's begin to clear our minds. . . .

Our Meditation

Please find a quiet place where you won't be disturbed for at least 15 minutes. Turn off the phone, play some soft music, and sit in a comfortable chair. It helps to wear loose, unrestricted clothing as well. The general principle in meditation is to sit upright, with the least amount of strain on your muscles and joints. By choosing this posture, your body can relax, and your meditation won't be hindered by physical discomfort. I find it helpful to uncross my legs and keep both feet on the floor.

It's best to have an intention before you start your meditation—whether it's to develop your awareness or to just let go of the day and check in with yourself. You can choose whatever intention you like because this is *your* time. Let's begin.

Close your eyes and simply focus on your breath. Breathe into your stomach slowly, and let the air move up to your lower lungs and then into the chest area. This is known as the "complete breath." Take it slow and easy. Each breath in will bring more and more relaxation, and each exhalation will let go of all stress and tension. Just do this for five minutes, lightly focusing on the regular rhythm of your breathing. Soon, you will naturally be more and more relaxed with every breath. Your breath is your instructor—trust that your next one will come without any effort. Just let it happen. Let it all go, and relax. If your mind starts to wander, just bring it back to your breath. Let your thoughts come in, acknowledge them, and slowly watch them leave again. Notice how it feels to be completely relaxed. Focus on your breath while you let all that mind chatter slow down and evaporate.

In your mind's eye, or third eye, I want you to imagine a symbol of your choosing. It can be a flower, a religious figure or icon, a word, or whatever is pleasing to you. Make it your own special symbol that you use every single time you meditate. At this point, just focus without straining on your symbol. I want you to inhale with a complete breath and bring your awareness up to your third eye as you focus on your symbol. It's almost as if you're breathing in and out through this center. Do this for another five minutes. If your mind wanders, focus on the breath and your symbol to bring you back.

During this relaxed state, it would be a great time to ask Spirit for an answer to a certain question. You can even ask if there's anything that your intuition has been trying to tell you. You may see an image, a scene, or beautiful colors. You can also allow your spirit guides to make themselves known to you. Your answer may not be immediate—it may even present itself in a few days. Or you could be at the right place, at the right time,

*and receive your answer immediately. After about
15 minutes, slowly move your fingers while re-
maining aware of your body, and bring yourself
back into the here-and-now and become aware
of the room around you. Remain seated for a
moment, contemplate your meditation, and see
how you feel.*

Meditation is an amazing practice because it's filled with many wonderful surprises. If you meditate before you go to sleep at night, a dream will often come to provide you with answers. For this reason, it's always helpful to keep a journal handy after you meditate and when you wake up in the morning. I suggest that you write down everything you feel when you first open your eyes—before your feet even touch the floor. Do this before your mind brings you back into full waking consciousness.

The Way of the Rose

Another type of meditation I have my students experiment with is "The Rose Meditation." You can try this with a friend. Have them tell you the name of someone they know whom they've been in contact with recently. It's better if you don't know the person they have in mind so you can be objective.

Next, go into your meditation, but instead of focusing on your symbol, picture a rose in your third eye (choose whatever color rose you wish), and concentrate on the person's name you were just given. Notice if the rose is opening and blooming . . . or is it slowly closing? Is it wilting, or is simply just bending? The rose will give you a clue as to how that person is doing in their life. If the rose is opening, you'll know that they're in a happy space right now. If it's wilting, then maybe they're going through an emotional time. Let your own intuitive awareness interpret what the rose means for that person.

Explain what you've received to your partner so they can confirm if you're on target. This is a great way to start trusting and stretching your abilities. It's only through practice that you'll be able to discriminate between your psychic self and your imagination.

Telepathy Exercises

To experience your own spirit communication, you should educate and experiment with the workings of telepathy. This shouldn't be too difficult, since we all possess this ability already, although most of us don't know it.

To help you, I'd like to share some exercises that I use with students in my workshops. Please realize that some people are better senders than receivers—you truly need to work on this skill to hone your own abilities.

Okay, let's practice! First, find a friend who's willing to help you and who might also be interested in developing their own psychic abilities. If you can find a class on this topic or an awareness group taught by an experienced teacher, then you're really on the right track.

Use the meditation mentioned earlier to still your mind before you begin. Also, have a pen and paper ready so that you can write down everything you're receiving. Although these exercises may seem simple, don't fool yourself. You'll be using a form of energy that we humans have moved away from—you'll need it to retrain your psychic mind.

In my classes, I usually divide the room in half and show a photo to one group of students—it might be a boat on a serene lake or a picture of a roller coaster. Each side then takes turns sending and receiving the images and the emotions that go with them.

You can also try this at home. Relax, and have fun with this exercise. You and your partner should take turns sending and receiving different images from pictures you clip out of a magazine. Sit back-to-back in chairs, and try to pick up the colors and textures of the image. I also want you to feel the emotion that goes with the picture. Ask your psychic self these questions: *Am I calm as I'm focusing, or is there an intense feeling? Are there any people in the picture? Are they indoors or outdoors?* After a few moments, you'll see how your mind picked up the image in its own unique way. Next, you should switch with your partner and let them try it.

You may also have your partner place different photos in envelopes, which they then pass to you. Your job is to write down what images and feelings you're picking up. Don't hesitate and change your mind. I want you to write down your first impressions. Telepathy is simply a tool. Don't be discouraged if you don't get many right at first— this is like any other skill that requires practice, patience, and experimentation. If you give it time, you'll be able to stretch and strengthen your spiritual abilities and stay connected forever with those in your life and those who have gone on before you.

◎

Spirits are constantly trying to send you signals to let you know that they're fine. It could be their favorite song playing on the radio at the exact moment you need to hear from them, you may smell their perfume or cologne, or simply just sense them. They'll also come through to you in your dreams, which is when the door to the Other Side is open and your conscious mind is taking a break. Watch for small signals and so-called coincidences, for they could be the spirits' biggest opportunities to say "Hello" or "I love you."

My last piece of advice is this: Keep an open mind, and read all you can about the gifts of the spirit. Realize that you're born with your own unique and special talents. I know that some of you are saying, "But I don't know what mine are!" Go back to your childhood and ask yourself what you loved then or what your passion is now. God gave each and every one of you individual talents to develop and share with others. That's your special gift—your signature on the world.

Mediumship is just one of these gifts, but there are so many others—writing, music, art, inspiration, and love, for example. And you're all capable of so much more. What you do with what you have is truly what matters. Seek your own experiences, and you'll attain your own awareness. In turn, you'll be able to make up your own mind about how you want to follow your own spiritual path.

God bless you. I wish you well. Enjoy the journey called *life,* for it's the most precious gift of all.

EPILOGUE
Night Sky

IT WAS A COOL SUMMER EVENING, and I was driving through the lush green countryside of New Hampshire on my way to Massachusetts, where I was to have one of my group sessions. All of a sudden, I heard the following words in my head: "It's an anniversary! It's an anniversary!" This message made a bit of sense to me because I was about to meet with eight people who hoped to connect with their friends and relatives in the spirit world. Judging from the joyful words that were coming to me on the I-95 Freeway, it was obvious that one spirit was extra eager to pick up the "phone" and talk to their loved one.

I knew that someone was about to get a special message, and that made me happy. As I gazed out the car window, I counted my blessings and felt thankful that my mom's health was better—she's now 72, living in Boston, and extremely proud of her "medium" son. And even though my parents had separated when I was a young man, that didn't mean I wanted to lose track of my father. Although I struggled with him when I was a boy, my adult self decided to reestablish a relationship with Dad, who's now 64 and living in New Hampshire.

I always loved my father, but the disease of alcoholism is so destructive—and not just to the drinker. It also affects the family, co-workers, and friends of the one lifting a glass, and its legacy can leave long-lasting effects. There was a lot of pain in my family, but I made a conscious decision as I got older not to blame my father. I decided to get on with my life instead of living in the past forever.

Forgiveness can be a beautiful thing, and I encourage anyone who has an alcoholic person in their lives to reach out and seek guidance and help. There are so many support groups to choose from that allow you to share your experiences and benefit from the strength of the group. You don't have to endure this ordeal alone. You can follow the natural progression from hurting to healing—and finally, to helping.

I'm happy to report that my father has been sober for many years—but that's not the only miracle. Recently, he's begun to call me with questions about his own life that have required my psychic skills to answer. What was once foreign and strange to him has provided comfort in his life. It's funny how things can come full circle . . . and through many long and frank talks, my father and I now understand each other.

I'm close to my two brothers and two sisters who live nearby, and I like to invite them to demonstrations so they can see their brother do his "thing." A few weeks ago, as I was finishing writing this book, I looked into the audience at a demonstration to see one of my brothers' handsome faces smiling back at me. When the session ended, I overheard him telling members of the audience, "You know who that is up there? That's my brother."

As for my other passion, I still love to draw, and now I dabble in other forms of art, including pottery and charcoal sketching. Art gets me out of my head and takes me to another place. It's also useful in my work. If I don't understand an image I'm seeing, I'll start to draw it and then show my client. I love it when they say, "Oh, that's the old staircase in Grandma's house."

I now have many clients, and most are even willing to wait months to see me. Due to this waiting list, I have a weekly group session as a way for me to reach out to as many people as possible. It's also quite a touching way for me to do my work: With a small, intimate group, it isn't just about the messages, but also about people coming together and bonding. In these settings, you can't hold back the loud bursts of laughter or the quiet tears as strangers become friends while absorbing themselves in the miracle that is someone else's life.

And so, on this night, I was meeting with one such group—this time at Circles of Wisdom, a charming meta-physical bookstore and gift shop in Andover, Massachusetts. Walking through the store, I couldn't suppress a smile, because I just knew that the message I'd heard in my car about the anniversary would be explained soon.

On rare occasions, I'm inspired to bring a gift to a group or demonstration and present it to the recipient of a message. Tonight was clearly one of those nights, and as usual, I didn't know exactly what I was supposed to bring until I felt drawn to a certain object. In the past, I've given stuffed animals, flowers, crystals, an angel, and even a silver dollar. The gift I bring is always for one person, who will know when they receive it that it belongs to them. There's always a special reason behind its presentation, and occasionally, I don't even get in on the why. But then again, I love the question marks as much as the answers.

As I wandered around the bookstore, I had so many choices in front of me, including cards, books, chimes, and posters. I walked slowly around while I waited for a sign. As

I strolled past the front counter, a certain item caught my eye, and I felt compelled to pick it up and feel it.

"Isn't that lovely?" the sales clerk asked. "We just received the shipment yesterday, and we only have two of them left."

Very strong energy told me that this was it. After asking the clerk to wrap it up, I left the present with my assistant, Gretchen. "I think this will be for someone this evening," I told her with a wink.

The group began, and two hours later, I still hadn't heard another word about the anniversary. Soon, I felt myself linking for what would certainly be the last message of the evening, and I knew we'd be having a very special connection.

As I looked around the room, I spotted Suzanne, a quiet, 50ish, blonde-haired woman in jeans and a T-shirt, who was the only person of the eight who hadn't received a message thus far. So I asked her, "Who's Fred?"

In the most hesitant way, Suzanne looked at me and gave me a barely discernible nod. She made it clear that she wasn't buying into one simple name. Luckily, more information was coming in to back it up. Words started to form on my lips, and I asked her, "Who's Lori? Laura? Lorelei?"

Suzanne's head popped up, and in a surprised voice, she said, "Did you say Lorelei?"

"That's not a common name—I'm wondering if you understand it," I responded.

"Yes, I do!" she exclaimed, choosing at that moment not to explain it any further. Suddenly, I knew this one was going to be a challenge.

"Who would have been known for the hats? Someone keeps putting these hats in front of me. I think it's a baseball cap," I said.

Looking down, a visibly upset Suzanne whispered, "My son, Matt, always wore baseball caps. He wouldn't be seen without one. "

"Your son has passed?" I asked.

She nodded.

"He passed very quickly, correct? And he's been gone about a year," I said.

A soft sob escaped Suzanne. Her best friend, who had been sitting next to her the entire evening, reached out to grab her hand for comfort and support. When she could compose herself, Suzanne said, "He did pass in a very fast way, on a motorcycle. He was only 22 years old. . . . It happened a year ago yesterday."

In my head, I realized one simple fact: *I have the anniversary.* But since she was so upset, I decided to go very slowly with Suzanne. I wanted to establish the link in the strongest possible way, so I decided to confirm a little bit more background information. "Who's Fred?" I asked her again.

"My husband!" she exclaimed.

"And now please tell me about this Lorelei," I said. "She was very close to Matt, and I feel that she helped him during his time here."

Suzanne told the group that her beloved son had had multiple sclerosis his entire life, and he went from a wheelchair to a walker to a cane to—unbelievably—walking on his own and even riding around on a motorcycle. Due to Matt's determination and the help of Lorelei, his physical therapist, he was able to defy the odds.

At this point, I allowed Suzanne a moment to absorb the evidence, and I addressed the rest of the group. "Everybody, I'd like to tell you a little story of my own. Sometimes I'm inspired to bring a small gift to these groups, although I never know who's supposed to receive it. On my way here tonight,

I did purchase something, because I kept hearing three words over and over again," I said as all eyes were transfixed on me. "I heard: 'It's an anniversary! It's an anniversary!'

"Now I know that this gift is for Suzanne," I said, as Gretchen handed me the small package wrapped in lavender tissue.

To Suzanne, I said, "Before I give you this present, I need to know one more thing: What does the word *star* mean to you?"

Suzanne began to weep. A few moments later, in a shaky voice, she explained to the group, "One of Matt's favorite things was to look for shooting stars. The night before he passed, we were at our summer house, which was always a special place for us. It has a long, weathered, wooden dock, and we sat down on the damp planks that night, dangled our feet, and looked up at the heavens.

"Last night, on the anniversary of Matt's death, I went out on our dock to look at the night sky with his girlfriend in the hopes of feeling close to Matt again," Suzanne said.

"Mom, your son wants to thank you for celebrating his life, and he wants to show you how much he loves you and is still with you," I said. "He also wants you to know that sometimes you *can* catch a shooting star."

A wistful smile spread across her face as I placed the lavender tissue in her trembling hands. "Can you please open your gift now?" I said softly.

Almost in slow motion, Suzanne began to lift each wisp of paper until she held up an almost perfect rose-quartz star. Suzanne gasped, as did most members of the group who watched the star twinkle in the glow of the candlelight in the room.

"This is Matt's," I said. "He picked it out for you. He wants you to know that he'll always be with you."

Later, Suzanne would tell me that this was the first time in a long time she'd felt at peace. Ever since, that star has topped her Christmas tree, as a reminder of Matt and his love.

These stories amaze me at times, yet I also realize that such wonder is always around us—we can experience it if we just open our minds and hearts.

Matt proved something else to me: Angels don't just fly . . . they also shine.

RECOMMENDED READING

Andrews, Ted. *How to Heal with Color,* Llewellyn Publications, 1999.

Burns, Litany. *The Sixth Sense of Children,* New American Library, 2002.

Edward, John. *Crossing Over: The Stories Behind the Stories,* Princess Books, 2001.

Guggenheim, Bill and Judy. *Hello from Heaven,* Bantam Books, 1995.

Hamilton-Parker, Craig. *The Psychic Workbook,* Vermilion, 1995.

Hoffman, Enid. *Develop Your Psychic Skills,* Para Research, 1981.

Judith, Anodea. *Wheels of Life,* Llewellyn Publication, 1999.

Northrop, Suzane. *Second Chance,* Jodere Group, 2002.

O'Brien, Stephen. *Angels by My Side,* Voices, 1994.

Payne, Phoebe. *Mankind's Latent Powers,* Pilgrim Books, 1992.

Ramacharaka, Yogi. *Science of Breath,* Kessinger Publishing Co., 1997.

Rando, Therese. *How to Go on Living When Someone You Love Dies,* Bantam, 1991.

Robinson, Lynn. *Compass of the Soul,* Andrews McMeel, 2003.

Sanders, Pete. *You Are Psychic!,* Ballantine Books, 1989.

Smith, Gordon. *Inner Visions,* Pembridge Publishing, 2000.

Williamson, Linda. *Contacting the Spirit World,* Piatkus, 1996.

UK RESOURCES

Arthur Findlay College
Stansted Hall
Stansted
CM24 8UD
England
Phone: + 44 (0)127 981 3636
E-mail: afc@snu.org.uk
www.arthurfindlaycollege.org

S.A.G.B (Spiritualist Association of Great Britain)
33 Belgrave Square
London
SW18QB
England
Phone: +44 (0) 207 235 3351

ABOUT THE AUTHOR

JOHN HOLLAND IS AN INTERNATIONALLY renowned psychic medium who has spent more than 20 years investigating and developing his abilities as a psychic medium.

John regularly lectures on both the East and West Coasts, and his public demonstrations provide his audience with a unique glimpse into the fascinating subject of mediumship, which he discusses in his uniquely humorous style, combined with his pure intensity and compassion. John's caring nature provides consistent counseling and support to his clients as he helps them connect with loved ones who have passed away, often bringing them a sense of closure and healing.

As a psychic medium, John's work has been featured on TV in *Unsolved Mysteries,* and he has also been interviewed on *Extra* and the Telemundo channel.

To contact the author:

www.JohnHolland.com
www.psijohn.com

ABOUT CINDY PEARLMAN

CINDY PEARLMAN IS A NATIONALLY syndicated writer for the *New York Times Syndicate* and the *Chicago Sun-Times.* Her work has appeared in *Entertainment Weekly, Premiere, People, Ladies' Home Journal, McCall's, Seventeen, Movieline,* and *Cinescape.* Over the past 15 years, she has interviewed Hollywood's biggest stars, who appear in her column "The Big Picture." Cindy is also the co-author of *Simple Things* (with Jim Brickman) and *It's Not about the Horse* (with Wyatt Webb).

— ◎ —

We hope you enjoyed this Hay House book.
If you would like to receive a free catalog featuring additional
Hay House books and products, or if you would like informa-
tion about the Hay Foundation, please contact:

Hay House, Inc.
P.O. Box 5100
Carlsbad, CA 92018-5100

(760) 431-7695 or (800) 654-5126
(760) 431-6948 (fax) or (800) 650-5115 (fax)
www.hayhouse.com

◎

Published and distributed in Australia by: Hay House Australia
Pty Ltd, P.O. Box 515, Brighton-Le-Sands, NSW 2216 • *phone:*
1800 023 516 • *e-mail:* info@hayhouse.com.au

Distributed in the United Kingdom by: Airlift, 8 The Arena,
Mollison Ave., Enfield, Middlesex,
United Kingdom EN3 7NL

Distributed in Canada by: Raincoast, 9050 Shaughnessy St.,
Vancouver, B.C., Canada V6P 6E5

— ◎ —